The Trinitarian Dance

The Trinitarian Dance

How the Triune God Develops Transformational Leaders

SHARON TAM

Foreword by Leighton Ford

WIPF & STOCK · Eugene, Oregon

THE TRINITARIAN DANCE
How the Triune God Develops Transformational Leaders

Copyright © 2015 Sharon Tam. All rights reserved. Except for brief quotations in critical publications or reviews, no part of this book may be reproduced in any manner without prior written permission from the publisher. Write: Permissions, Wipf and Stock Publishers, 199 W. 8th Ave., Suite 3, Eugene, OR 97401.

Wipf & Stock
An imprint of Wipf and Stock Publishers
199 W. 8th Ave., Suite 3
Eugene, OR 97401

www.wipfandstock.com

ISBN 13: 978-1-62564-557-9

Chapter 4 contains Roger Nicole's diagram to preserve the doctrine of the Trinity, found in Nicole's *Standing Forth: The Collected Writings of Roger Nicole* (Fearn, Ross-shire, Scotland: Christian Focus, 2002), 389–396. Reprinted with permission of the editor of Christian Focus.

Chapter 8 contains a slightly revised version of Shirley Guthrie's Figure C: The Fellowship of the Father, Son, and Holy Spirit, found in Guthrie's *Christian Doctrine*, rev. ed. (Louisville: Westminster John Knox, 1994), 92. Reprinted with permission of the editor of Westminster John Knox.

All Scripture quotations are from The Holy Bible, New International Version®, NIV® Copyright © 1973, 1978, 1984, 2011 by Biblica, Inc.™ Used by permission. All rights reserved worldwide.

Manufactured in the U.S.A.

Contents

List of Figures | vii
List of Abbreviations | ix
Foreword by Leighton Ford | xi
Introduction | xiii

Part 1: The State of Leadership in the Canadian Church

1 Why the Trinitarian Dance? | 3
2 Belonging in Canada | 19
3 Behaving in Canada | 29

Part 2: A Theology of the Trinitarian Leadership Dance

4 The Trinitarian Dance as a Model for Transformational Leadership Development | 41
5 Movement I: Demonstration | 66
6 Movement II: Choreography | 80
7 Movement III: Orchestration | 98
8 Movement IV: Performance | 110

Part 3: Church-Based Strategies for the Trinitarian Leadership Dance

9 The Trinitarian Dance of Leader Development in the Local Church | 125
10 An Invitation from the Triune God | 143

Bibliography   153

Figures

Figure 1. Shield of the Trinity | 45

Figure 2. Three Heresies Avoided by the Early Church | 46

Figure 3. The Traditional Symbol for the Trinity | 112

Figure 4. A Symmetrical Model of the Trinity | 112

Figure 5. Andrei Rublev's Holy Trinity | 113

Figure 6. The Trinitarian Leadership Dance | 127

Abbreviations

BDAG   Walter Bauer, Frederick W. Danker, W. F. Arndt, and F. W. Gingrich. *Greek- English Lexicon of the New Testament and Other Early Christian Literature.* 2nd ed. Chicago: University of Chicago Press, 1979.

BDB   Francis Brown, S. R. Driver, and Charles A. Briggs. *Hebrew and English Lexicon of the Old Testament.* Oxford: Clarendon, 1951.

TWOT   *Theological Wordbook of the Old Testament.* Edited by R. Laird Harris, Gleason L. Archer Jr., and Bruce K. Waltke. Chicago: Moody, 1980.

Foreword

Leadership, like life, has its seasons. And seasons have their moods . . . winter often grayer, spring livelier, summer flourishing, autumn flaming and aging. So, as leaders, we are called to pursue our calling in the different seasons of our lives, and the varying stages of our ministries.

Sometimes as leaders we feel we are plodding—as if wearing snowshoes and tiredly shifting on a step at a time—trying not to give up. At other times we sense we are racing—as if skating across a frozen river or down the Rideau Canal—almost out of breath—exhilarated but almost in danger of losing our balance.

Leadership also is affected not only by pace, but by the shifting light of the seasons. Light, it has been said, has two opposites: darkness, and heaviness. Leadership has its dark side. It can also be very heavy, and burdensome.

Yet Jesus promised to his disciples a burden that is "light"—because he shares it with us. We must shun (like the devil) leadership "lite"—following the latest leadership fashions. But we should seek (like Jesus!) leadership "light"—leading like, with, and to Jesus.

Years ago I read, in a piece by Vern Eller, I think, that the "image of God" can be conceived of as a dance—a dance with God as the lead partner, we the ones who sense his movement and go with his lead. I am glad that Sharon Tam has picked up this image of the dance as a defining image of leadership.

Trinitarian theology helps us to live our lives and practice our leadership shaped not just by the norms of our cultures or the shape of our personalities or the demands of our institutional seasons, but in the rhythm of the Triune God—whose timing is unpredictable, but never too early or too late, always "just in time."

So as disciples, leaders in our families and churches and society, may we listen and join in to the Voice that calls, "May I have this dance"!

Leighton Ford
Charlotte, North Carolina

Introduction

The Canadian church is suffering due to an inadequate appreciation of the mystery of the Triune God, an apathetic culture, and underdeveloped leaders. It needs leaders who are securely rooted in God's love, equipped with his vision and values, and trained with the transformational leadership principles that are embodied in the Holy Trinity. This book is a clarion call for leaders to approach their life and leadership in a *perichoretic* fashion, that is, in a way that best reflects the dance and love of the Triune God. The goal is for leaders to identify where they are lacking, to understand the timeless movements and steps of the Trinitarian Dance, to partner with the Triune God in developing a unique leadership dance within their particular context, and to train others to do the same.

To develop a successful strategy of leadership development in Canadian churches, leaders must assess where they are and where they are called to go. For this reason, Part 1 examines the gap between the reserved and dispassionate reality of Canadian Christians and the desired outcome of self-initiating, reproducing, passionate, transformational leaders. Chapter 1 contrasts a Canadian identity and its values of pluralism, relativism, and secularism with a Christian identity based on mutual respect, true tolerance, and a commitment to the truth. Chapter 2 compares a fractured sense of individualism and isolation with the biblical portrait of authentic community. Chapter 3 distinguishes between Canadians' disengagement with society and Christ's invitation to join in God's mission of transformation.

The second part of this book provides a rationale for using the Trinitarian Dance as a model for training leaders. Chapter 4 explores the biblical, foundational, and practical nature of the Trinity; paints a picture of God's mysterious dance and how the members of the Trinity relate with one another; and unpacks three preliminary truths based on each member of the Trinity. Chapters 5–8, respectively, describe the four movements of

Introduction

the Trinity's leadership dance: demonstration, choreography, orchestration, and performance. Within each movement, there are three leadership steps, which are danced by each member of the Trinity throughout biblical history. Apprentices of the Trinity need to learn these twelve steps, practice them, and then dance them creatively to bring about lasting transformation.

The final section of this discussion presents church-based strategies for leadership development. Chapter 9 helps leaders to master the four movements by practicing the twelve steps and to celebrate their unique calling and giftedness, bringing about transformation in their own context. Chapter 10 concludes with a doxology of praise to the Trinity and a benediction of grace, hope, and love for the future.

It is my ongoing prayer and hope for Canada to be transformed by the living, risen Christ and to fulfill its God-given destiny as a nation. In order to do so, leaders must be equipped to bring about authentic transformation. The Trinitarian Dance described in this book is a model that will encourage you to examine character issues, expose you to leadership essentials, and empower you with leadership tools and disciplines. Above all, it will bring you closer to God's heart and vision for all to be caught up in the Trinitarian dance of love with God, with one another, and with the world.

PART 1

The State of Leadership in the Canadian Church

1

Why the Trinitarian Dance?

Imagine the Trinity as a parent who picks up and embraces a young child, spinning him around and around and around. Picture the joy and laughter of the child, the delight of the parent watching the child, and the both of them enjoying life together. Playing, laughing, enjoying one another's company—these verbs do not usually describe the task of leadership, yet they are the essence of following the triune God. Leaders should not be denied such childlike faith, laughter, and enjoyment. A deeper understanding of the Trinitarian Dance reveals certain steps and rhythms that captivate, motivate, and transform as leaders participate in the dance with God.

The Trinitarian Dance approach to leadership development comes out of a conviction that the Trinity is foundational to Christian leadership. When I began researching this book, I had only a dim awareness of trinitarian theology and the current academic interest in the Trinity. Little did I realize that the Trinity was inviting me into a deeper investigative journey: probing the glorious mysteries of his inner life and exploring how that life reflects the leadership dance. The Trinity has been training me to dance in leadership with greater ease, more enjoyment, and increased impact. I want to share these movements and steps with you so that you might also experience greater ease, enjoyment, and impact in leadership. As dancers learn to move lightly and avoid stumbling over their feet, a Trinitarian Dance paradigm equips leaders to avoid being overburdened by duties and tripping over concerns. By dancing in your world with the triune God, you will be embraced and empowered to bring about authentic and lasting transformation, and resourced to train others to do the same.

The Trinity can be likened to three people dancing together in a circular pattern. Their movements are so intertwined that an observer cannot distinguish one dancer from another. Similarly, the Father, Son, and Holy Spirit dance through, around, and with one another, exuding a dynamic and creative energy that continually transforms, and ultimately restores, all of creation. This is the Trinitarian Dance. We are invited into this dynamic, creative, and joyous movement as dance partners with the triune God of love. But we have been crippled, deeply scarred, and wounded by a cataclysmic fall, ripped from the arms of our loving dance partner. We need Jesus to come, pick us up, and teach us how to dance again: effortlessly, creatively, and joyously. So often we stumble out of step with the dance of God, but in the Trinity we are invited to join in it once again, to choreograph our steps, and then to invite others to dance with us.

The church needs the Trinitarian Dance because the bride of Christ is crippled, hurting, tattered, bruised, and wounded, earnestly desiring to dance but not knowing how. Many have become disconnected from the Head of the Body, unable to hear his still small voice in the noise of distractions, and forgetting the song of the dance in the pursuit of success. Members of the clergy now suffer from obesity, hypertension, and depression at rates higher than most other professions. In the last decade, statistics for pastors and Christian leaders in Canada have shown that the use of antidepressants has risen, while life expectancy has fallen among pastors and leaders. Many would change jobs if they could, and often leaders have no close friends in their immediate and daily contexts.

The Trinitarian Dance introduces a fresh approach. The motif of dance is used to frame essential leadership practices, principles, and skills. It is a model of leadership development that includes four major movements: demonstration, choreography, orchestration, and performance. Each movement begins with three steps. These steps and movements are not linear; rather, they are like recurring rhythms and motifs. As you learn to listen for and recognize the rhythms and motifs in the triune God's song of love, you might feel your foot starting to tap and your soul starting to sway. Soon you will not be able to stay put because your dance partner invites you to rise and receive his embrace, practice the steps, join the dance, and invite others to join in as well. The triune God will guide you on a unique and exciting journey where you will need the flexibility, creativity, and ease of a trinitarian leadership dance to shine Christ's light and hope in a dark and hurting world. In the process, your relationship with the Trinity will result in greater joy, laughter, creativity, and delight, and lead you to astonishing outcomes.

The experience of North American church leaders, however, does not always mirror the ease, joy, and delight of an adventure with a dancing God. More importantly, the resultant effect on the church is disappointing. Attendance is down in many churches across North America. Secularism has displaced Judeo-Christian values and morality from the "public square" and set up its own ideologies. Leaders, who genuinely desire renewal, have largely abandoned the current ecclesiastical structures.[1] While there are small pockets of renewal, leaders rarely exhibit the joy, peace, and love found in the dance of God. The Trinitarian Dance offers a timely, practical, and much-needed response to these disappointing realities.

While there are many similarities between American and Canadian landscapes, there are some unique challenges for the Canadian church as it engages in the Trinitarian Dance. According to a survey done in 2003 in the Canadian church, many clergy have expressed general dissatisfaction (frustration, stress, anxiety, and anger) in their ministry.[2] Essentially, they feel relationally unfulfilled and lonely. The study also has shown that 60 percent have considered leaving ministry, and a considerable number (16 percent) indicated that they have suffered from depression (double the national rate).[3] Many leaders and pastors are struggling, ill equipped to deal with the challenges of the Canadian milieu. What is it about Canada that makes ministry particularly challenging in ways that are not shared by our U.S. counterparts?

BEING CANADIAN

What exactly does a distinctly Canadian identity look like? Does it mean that one says "eh" after every second sentence, uses the slogan "I am Canadian,"[4] drinks Tim Horton's coffee or Molson's beer, and listens to Justin Bieber? Do moose, beavers, Canadian geese, or loons evoke a sense of national pride? Must one read Margaret Atwood, wear a toque, use maple

1. Viola, *Reimagining Church*.
2. Irvine, "Clergy Well-Being," 7–10.
3. Ibid., 11.
4. "I am Canadian" is the popular, well-known slogan of Canada's national beer.

Part 1: The State of Leadership in the Canadian Church

syrup on pancakes, play ice hockey, and fly either the maple leaf or the *fleur-de-lis* flag in order to be patently Canadian? Not really. Many do none of the above yet are bona fide citizens of this great nation. A uniquely Canadian identity as a unified subject is an elusive concept, due both to Canada's multiculturalism[5] and its multilingualism,[6] yet there are a few characteristics that distinguish Canada from the rest of the world.

Americans often describe Canadians as nice, yet, when pressed for other qualities, they pause, and repeat, "Canadians are . . . well . . . nice"— they cannot think of anything else to say![7] There is a shortage of people, both in the church and in Canadian society, who will take initiative, stand firm for moral values, and work faithfully for positive change. Canadians are not usually in the forefront of global concerns, social justice issues, or challenging the status quo. This reality is perhaps the reason for the leadership vacuum in the Canadian church. Canadians, in general, do not relish being in the forefront of anything. If I were to call the Canadian church to repent of a single reality, it would be, in one word, apathy.[8]

THE GLARING CANADIAN SYMPTOM: APATHY

Apathy masquerades in many different forms. It could be defined as indifference, describing people who are unresponsive to various aspects of life. It is marked by a lack of emotion, motivation, and enthusiasm. Apathy is very similar to laziness and even could be considered an extreme form of it. In Canada, apathy presents itself as tolerance, blending in, and autonomy— three Canadian values that reflect Canadian beliefs, sense of belonging, and behavior. Canadian Christians need to reclaim the true meaning of these values and demonstrate to Canadians a lifestyle of true tolerance, blending into authentic community, and being free to do what is right.

---

5. Bibby, *Bibby Report*, 36. Canada passed the *Official Languages Act* in 1969 and the *Canadian Multiculturalism Act* in 1988.

6. Now, with the establishment of the new province of Nunavut (one of whose official languages is Inuktitut), Canada formally recognizes multilingualism. Adams et al., *Fire and Ice*, 124.

7. Middleton, "Perspectives on the World Christian Movement."

8. I am not alone in my conclusions. In 1990, Vision 2000 and Outreach Canada clearly saw these realities in the Canadian context and called for repentance as follows: "What is needed is repentance of apathy, prayerlessness, and disunity, together with a fresh commitment to obedience to our Lord as we seek to re-evangelize Canada." Moerman, "Church Planting," 96.

Examples of Canadian apathy can be seen everywhere in Canada. Many see Canada's delivery of products and services as second-rate. Canadian conferences pale in comparison to their neighbors to the south. Canadian companies have difficulties competing globally. Scholarship in Canada is minimal in its contributions to the larger academic community. Canadians are apathetic when it comes to politics, as shown by the low voter turnout during elections.[9] Moreover, Canada demands very little of its new citizens, except to swear allegiance to the Queen, faithfully observe the laws of Canada, and fulfill their duties as citizens; however, nowhere are those duties defined or even enforced.[10] When it was discovered that Michäelle Jean, the former Governor General of Canada and de facto head of state, held dual citizenship with France, few Canadians seemed to care.[11] Canadians must awaken from their apathy and produce world-class leaders who will advance God's mission both in Canada and around the world.

APATHY AS TOLERANCE: A CANADIAN CORE BELIEF

Canada is a country that highly values tolerance but has been misled into an understanding of tolerance as agreement with ideas and values with which one intrinsically disagrees. Tolerance, by definition, does not imply agreement. Yet, postmodernity has underminded the Canadian quest for truth. As such, Canadians believe they ought to agree with any and all faiths regardless of a concern for truth, goodness, and rightness. Consequently, no strong national identity exists, nor does any strong religious tradition guide the Canadian consciousness. The concept of absolute truth has become completely discarded. This section explains the social realities of the Canadian context in an effort to understand why Canadians value tolerance, how we have been misguided, and how we can return to true tolerance.

---

9. Elections Canada, "Voter Turnout at Federal Elections and Referendums, 1867–2006."

10. Cohen, *Unfinished Canadian*, 136–40.

11. Ibid., 141.

Part 1: The State of Leadership in the Canadian Church

Pluralism

Canada is a pluralistic society, embracing both a cultural and a religious pluralism. Pluralism is defined as "the condition in which numerous distinct ethnic, religious, or cultural groups are present and tolerated within a society. It also connotes the idea that such a condition is desirable or socially beneficial."[12] In fact, Canada has become an example to the world of how distinct cultural and religious groups can live together in peace and harmony. Reginald W. Bibby, Canada's leading sociologist, unpacks pluralism as follows: "Expressed globally, it means that war and domination of societies no longer are appropriate. Cultural obliteration in the form of intolerance and alleged enlightening is unacceptable. Customs and languages, worldviews and religions, are not to be tampered with."[13]

Pluralism is espoused as the ideal, but is it realistic, and does it genuinely contribute to the overall good of the society? Certainly, it is beneficial when religious and culturally distinct groups mutually respect and learn from one another. Yet, this mutuality is not what pluralism means to most Canadians. Rather, most have the false notion that pluralism means embracing and accepting all cultural and religious beliefs. While welcoming a variety of different cultures and beliefs within a society is very enriching, differing cultures and religious beliefs contain both good and bad elements and should not be embraced equally. There are elements of the Garden of Eden and of the fall of humanity in every culture. Likewise, accepting all religious beliefs without perspicacity has resulted in a denial of ultimate truth and deafness towards any truth claims.

Cultural Pluralism

While Canada may not have a very strong national identity, there is one aspect that is a source of pride and joy: the Canadian cultural mosaic. "Cultural mosaic" is a term used to describe Canada's multiculturalism.[14] Canada is, as former Prime Minister Joe Clark's government's slogan proclaimed, "a community of communities."[15] Often this diversity is as true within denominational affiliations as it is within the nation as a whole.

---

12. *Dictionary.com*, s.v. "pluralism."
13. Bibby, *Mosaic Madness*, 2.
14. "Canadian Multiculturalism."
15. Webber, *Reimagining Canada*, 106.

Why the Trinitarian Dance?

Bibby, who has worked extensively in surveying Canadians since 1975, confirms this: "There is perhaps no single characteristic that we are inclined to point to more in describing Canadian uniqueness than the fact that we are a cultural mosaic."[16] The philosophy of a mosaic stands in contrast to the United States' model of a melting pot as an assimilation strategy for different cultures. This reality means that Canadians are not "unarmed Americans in parkas . . . with health insurance"[17]; rather, they are people who are happy being Canadian, fond of their country, and proud of their cultural mosaic.[18]

The primary reason why Canadians like their country is because it is not part of the United States. In fact, the most salient feature of the Canadian national identity is that Canadians are "not-Americans." Even though Canadians perceive themselves as "nationally inferior" to their neighbors to the South,[19] they do not want to be like them. Canadians devote a great deal of energy insisting that they are "not-Americans," both in their own cultural products and when they travel outside North America and are frequently mistaken as coming from the United States. Unfortunately, this unwarranted prejudice towards their North American neighbors is a distinguishing characteristic of the Canadian identity. Canadians' disdain of the American melting pot philosophy, or anything else American, gives them a sense of pride in their own cultural mosaic. Somehow, due to the Multiculturalism Act, Canadians believe that they are more tolerant than their American neighbors.[20]

Religious Pluralism

Many confuse religious diversity with religious relativism and often equate these two distinct ideas with religious pluralism.[21] Religious diversity affirms the demographic reality of a society in which people of varied religious

---

16. Bibby, *Bibby Report*, 35.
17. Adams et al., *Fire and Ice*, x and 13.
18. Bibby, *Bibby Report*, 40–41.
19. In probing how Canadians feel about themselves, relative to how they feel about Americans, Bibby has observed that with respect to confidence, patriotism, risk-takers, the Americans win easily. Bibby, *Bibby Report*, 49.
20. *Canadian Multiculturalism Act*, R.S.C., 1985, c. 24 (4th Supp.). See also "The Canadian Multiculturalism Act."
21. *Stanford Encyclopedia of Philosophy*, "Religious Diversity (Pluralism)."

Part 1: The State of Leadership in the Canadian Church

backgrounds live together. Religious relativism assumes that all religions are equal and unequivocally true. One states that diverse ideas about faith exist and should exist; whereas the other pronounces that all faiths are good and helpful, contribute to a better society, and should be accepted equally. Religious pluralism is the assertion that one truth claim of faith is no truer than another. Brian C. Stiller notes, "Such a system of faith rejects even the possibility of a claim to truth."[22] This blurring between religious diversity and relativism has led to intolerance towards the exclusive claims of Christ. Canadian authorities and institutions use pluralism to prevent faith from exercising influence in Canada's public life.[23] In 1988 the Canadian government passed the Canadian Multiculturalism Act,[24] decreeing that what is "descriptively obvious" is now "prescriptively valued."[25] Postmodern voices now advocate for religious relativism on the basis of Canada's pluralism; however, the Multiculturalism Act does not sanction such a shift. The act states that "persons belonging to ethnic, religious or linguistic minorities shall not be denied the right to enjoy their own culture, to profess and practice their own religion or to use their own language."[26] In other words, the only aspect of Canadian life that the act affirms is cultural and religious diversity—not relativism.

Religious relativism is not beneficial, positive, or logical; it does not enhance society. As Gary Walsh points out, "It makes no sense to take a collection of contrary beliefs and assume that because we live in a pluralistic society, each belief must be true."[27] Not every belief is intrinsically right or good. For instance, if one believes that the only sure way to go to heaven is to kill infidels by blowing oneself up, this belief will not contribute to the overall good of society. Walsh adds, "Supporting the pluralistic idea that all religions have the right to exist and be free from discrimination is quite different from saying that we cannot debate and evaluate the claims of each religion to determine if they are legitimate or true."[28]

Unfortunately, instead of recognizing this distinction and confidently proclaiming the gospel alongside other religious faiths, most Christians

---

22. Stiller, *From the Tower of Babel to Parliament Hill*, 158.
23. Ibid., 157.
24. *Canadian Multiculturalism Act*, R.S.C., 1985, c. 24 (4th Supp.).
25. Bibby, *Mosaic Madness*, 7.
26. *Canadian Multiculturalism Act*, R.S.C., 1985, c. 24 (4th Supp.).
27. Walsh, "Striving for Relevance in a Changing Nation," 314.
28. Ibid.

believe that "a pluralistic society requires them to be silent about their own religious convictions."[29] This tendency to be silent has been accentuated by the Canadian Christian preference for privatized faith. In response to this, Stiller observes:

> My experience with people from other faiths is that they don't want expressions of Christian faith to be lost in our culture. As one person said, the reason he came to Canada was because Christianity had created a framework of fairness and openness. His conclusion? Now that he was here, why would he want Canada to be less Christian?[30]

Canadian Christians need to learn how to "unbutton their lips" and "wisely and winsomely occupy their seat at the diverse table of pluralistic society."[31] Church leaders must train and equip believers to "give permission to others to believe as they choose to believe while at the same time taking permission to believe what we believe."[32] This includes the proclamation of the gospel. Churches need to create safe places to discuss openly and ask questions about what Christians believe and why Christian beliefs and practices are important. To do so, it is important to explore further this shift in the cultural landscape towards relativism.

Relativism

Relativism has been accepted as a given in Canada, and any claims of absolute truth or discernment of what is considered best is often perceived as intolerant or bigoted. To relativists, there is no such thing as "the truth," but only "my truth" and "your truth." Relativism obscures any discussion of the truth. Stiller argues that the story of the blindfolded men describing an elephant, often used to argue for relativism, misses the point.[33] One person, holding the trunk, thinks it is a fire hose. Another, grasping onto the leg, believes it is a tree trunk. A third, touching the tail, perceives it to be a rope. Each is sure he knows the truth. The crazy conclusion is this: nothing is true because each perception is equally valid. The irony of the

---

29. Posterski, *Where's a Good Church*, 112.
30. Stiller, *From the Tower of Babel to Parliament Hill*, 156.
31. Stetson and Conti, *Truth about Tolerance*, 109.
32. Posterski, *Where's a Good Church*, 112.
33. Stiller, *From the Tower of Babel to Parliament Hill*, 159–60.

story however, is that everyone who hears the story knows the whole truth about the elephant.

The problem with relativism is that people are usually only relativistic when it comes to religious or moral values, especially when resisting traditional Judeo-Christian morality. Walsh cites Canadian apologist Michael Horner as saying, "We don't hear people claiming that mutually exclusive statements are true when it comes to the stock market."[34] Furthermore, the idea that relativism is exclusively and absolutely true is both contradictory[35] and intolerant. "It is no more tolerant than any other exclusive claim to the truth. In fact, it is worse—because it hides its claim to be the absolute truth behind the facade of denying the existence of absolute truth."[36] Sadly, most Canadians tacitly have bought into this cultural norm of relativism and the resultant moral ambiguity, centeredlessness, and anarchy that this philosophy generates. Bibby summarizes it well:

> Relativism has slain moral consensus, stripping us of our ethical and moral guidelines, leaving us with no authoritative instruments with which to measure social life. Our standards for evaluating ideas and behavior have been restricted to our local cultural and religious domains. We are a country that was a champion of choice, that we triumphantly discarded the idea that there are better and best choices in favor of worshipping choice as an end in itself.[37]

Secularism

The widespread acceptance of relativism has occurred due to secularism in both political and educational arenas. Since Canada has no dominant religion, secularists (using the arguments of relativism) have proceeded to gag the religious institutions that might oppose their political agenda. Since Canadians generally are reserved, peace loving, and affable in nature,

---

34. Walsh, "Striving for Relevance in a Changing Nation," 317.

35. The statement that "all is relative" is either a relative statement or an absolute one. If it is relative, then this statement does not rule out absolutes and provides for the possibility that Christianity is correct in its assertions. If the statement is absolute, on the other hand, then it proves itself false by using the word "all" and stands as an example of an absolute claim.

36. Walsh, "Striving for Relevance in a Changing Nation," 317.

37. Bibby, *Mosaic Madness*, 14.

Why the Trinitarian Dance?

they passively have turned a blind eye as secularism has displaced Judeo-Christian values and morality from the "public square"[38] and set up its own ideologies.[39] Don Posterski describes this sad reality in Canada: "In practice, rather than being *active atheists*, most Canadians are *passive theists*. This results in functional secularism."[40]

Many Canadians see secularism as the answer to religious pluralism, but there are two main problems with it: it is exclusive and intolerant. The secularists' rationale goes something like this: "In order to have harmony in an increasingly religiously pluralistic society, religion should be removed from the public arena and confined to private life—where it belongs." In other words, to give equal respect to all religions, society must exclude all of them from having a public role. So, in the aftermath of the terrible tragedy of the September 11, 2001 attacks on the United States World Trade Center and Pentagon, when people were crying out for comfort from a sovereign deity, Canada chose not to offer prayer or even to mention God's name on Parliament Hill. Instead, the country stood in silence. By accepting the preference of those who do not want religion, secularism excludes the preferences of all others. Yet, it is only one position alongside all others; it is only one way, not the only way.

The second problem with secularism is that it is intolerant toward any who oppose its position. In fact, secularists do not argue fairly against the Judeo-Christian worldview; rather, they "suppress that perspective from gaining a serious cultural hearing," ruling it out by labeling it "intolerant" or "narrow-minded."[41] Ironically, secularists make a lot of narrow-minded moral judgments, such as these: "Racism is wrong; failing to observe the separation of church and state is wrong; outlawing abortion is wrong; affirmative action [i.e., equity] is morally right; people should be tolerant, etc."[42] Secularists dismiss traditional morality on the grounds of relativism, yet the values and moral judgments adhered to by secularists are presented as objectively right, just, and fair based on the Canadian Charter of Rights and

---

38. Neuhaus, *Naked Public Square*.

39. Most notably was the Canadian's government's report, *Equality for All*, which recommended that no organization discriminate on the basis of religion or on the basis of sexual orientation; noted in Stackhouse, *Canadian Evangelicalism in the Twentieth Century*, 170.

40. Posterski, *Where's a Good Church*, 111.

41. Taylor, *Is God Intolerant?*, 53–55.

42. Stetson and Conti, *Truth about Tolerance*, 89.

Freedoms. It is a kind of "bait and switch,"[43] a "pluralist game"[44] in which relativism becomes the grounds upon which to reject Judeo-Christian values and morality; yet, the values and morality of secularism are promulgated on nonrelativistic grounds.

THE CANADIAN CHURCH: A LACK OF PASSION

Scripture paints a picture of the early church that is completely different from the picture of the Canadian church today.[45] Rather than indiscriminately accepting and embracing any and all beliefs and practices, believers in the early church mutually respected one another's opinions and patiently tolerated behavior and practices with which they disagreed. They resolutely committed to the truth of the resurrection, giving their lives for the sake of the gospel. They were bold in their witness of Christ's kingdom and passionate in their love for God. A comparison of the early church and the Canadian church today reveals glaring discrepancies.

True Tolerance

Believers in the early church were "critically tolerant" or "truly tolerant" of the various faith expressions and unbelief that they encountered, whereas Canadian believers are "hyper-tolerant" or "uncritically accepting" of any and every faith expression or unbelief that they encounter. "True tolerance" is simply this: "patience towards a practice or opinion one disapproves of."[46] It is important to notice that the idea behind tolerance contains the notion of disagreement. "If there is no disagreement, there is nothing to tolerate."[47] Hyper-tolerance, by contrast, is "legally permitting that which should not be permitted or praising that which is blameworthy or remaining silent toward an injustice."[48] Pluralism, relativism, and secularism have changed the definition of tolerance into "acceptance" and "respect." In other words,

---

43. Ibid., 90.

44. Canavan, *Pluralist Game*.

45. Ogden's "The Biblical Standard and the Current Reality" forms the backdrop for the comparisons made in chapters 1 through 3 regarding the Canadian church. Ogden, *Transforming Discipleship*, 24–38.

46. Stetson and Conti, *Truth about Tolerance*, 140.

47. Hamblin, "Evangelical Resources on True Tolerance."

48. Stetson and Conti, *Truth about Tolerance*, 152.

"tolerance has evolved from *abiding the objectionable* to *affirming the rightness* of the diverse and nontraditional [sic]."[49]

In the early church, wives with unbelieving husbands were instructed to "tolerate" their unbelief. This tolerance created an environment in which these wives could work towards winning their spouses over by their good deeds and inner beauty of a gentle spirit (1 Cor 7:13; 1 Pet 3:1–2). If an unbelieving spouse left, the believing one was to "tolerate" this behavior. This was advocated not because it was a good or right action but because God has called his people to live in peace (1 Cor 7:15).

Likewise, the Apostle Paul studied idol worship in Athens in order to reason with the Athenians and proclaim to them the truth for which they searched (Acts 17:16–23). He was well acquainted with Greek literature, philosophy, and art. He quoted Greek poets routinely (Acts 17:28; 1 Cor 15:33; Titus 1:12) not to embrace their worldview, but in an effort to persuade people to become believers of the living and risen Christ. His behavior displayed a "true tolerance" in understanding beliefs that were contrary to his own, yet he remained critical of the errors in these beliefs. Philip, in the same way, was able to listen and understand. He "tolerated" where a person was in his spiritual journey and sought to bring him to the place were he had the opportunity to receive God's gift of eternal life in Jesus Christ (Acts 8:26–40).

In contrast, Canadian Christians have "buttoned their lips" not only with regards to sharing their faith journey but also with regards to speaking up on moral issues. Desiring to avoid being perceived as narrow-minded, Christians have eschewed a "critical" or "true tolerance" in favor of the more socially acceptable "hyper-tolerance." What is needed is for Christian leaders to train and equip their church members to understand true tolerance and winsomely yet boldly share their own personal faith story. Church leaders must model and train others in personal witness. By developing or adopting a code of ethics for personal witness,[50] church leaders can educate congregations about what constitutes appropriate conversation that both respects people's individual beliefs and the exclusive claims of the gospel.

---

49. Ibid., 93.
50. InterVarsity Christian Fellowship, "Evangelism Code of Ethics."

Part 1: The State of Leadership in the Canadian Church

Rate yourself and the ministry in which you're involved on a scale of 1 to 4, with 1 being uncritically accepting to 4 being critically tolerant.		
Canadian Church Symptom	**My Rating**	**Ministry Rating**
1. Uncritically accepting other beliefs. 2. Tacitly accepting other beliefs. 3. Tacitly disagreeing with other beliefs. 4. Respectfully disagreeing with other beliefs.		

Commitment to the Truth

Another gap existing between the Canadian church and the biblical record lies in the core understanding of truth. The early Christians gave their lives because they believed the absolute truth of the resurrection. They relied on the complete trustworthiness of the gospel of Christ. By comparison, many Canadian Christians are not sure whether absolute truth even exists, let alone willing to give their lives for it.

Church history records that all the apostles, except for the Apostle John, were martyred for proclaiming the truth of the resurrection of Jesus Christ.[51] The early church was so convinced of the truth of the reality of God—as a loving heavenly Father, the living and risen Savior, and the presence and power of the Holy Spirit—that they boldly and confidently shared their faith wherever they went.[52] Paul even issued a challenge to the Corinthians to prove the resurrection of Jesus Christ false (1 Cor 15:13–19). He daringly asserted that if, at any time, anyone objectively could disprove the

---

51. According to *The Catholic Encylopedia*, Andrew was martyred by crucifixion (bound, not nailed, to a cross (s.v. "St. Andrew"); Bartholomew (also known as Nathaniel) was martyred by either being beheaded or flayed alive and crucified, head downward (s.v. "St. Bartholomew"); James, son of Zebedee (the Greater), was martyred by being beheaded or stabbed with a sword (Acts 12:2) (s.v. "St. James the Greater"); James, son of Alphaeus (the Lesser), was martyred by being thrown from a pinnacle of the Temple at Jerusalem, then stoned and beaten with clubs (s.v. "St. James the Less"); Jude (also know as Thaddeus) was martyred by being beaten to death with a club (s.v. "Jude Thaddeus"); Matthew was martyred by being burned, stoned, or beheaded (s.v. "St. Matthew"); Peter was martyred by being crucified with his head downwards in Rome (s.v. "St. Peter, Prince of the Apostles"); Philip was martyred (s.v. "St. Philip the Apostle"); Simon the Zealot was martyred by crucifixion or being sawn in half (s.v. "Simon the Apostle"); and Thomas was martyred by being stabbed with a spear (s.v. "St. Thomas the Apostle").

52. Although the doctrine of the Trinity wasn't officially formulated until the fourth century at the Council of Nicea, early believers experience the reality of the triune God through answered prayers, miracles, and the testimony of the apostles.

resurrection of Jesus Christ then he would concede that the Christian faith is false, utterly useless, and worthy to be discarded.

Today, the majority of Canadians (50 percent of adults and 67 percent of young people) believe that what is right and wrong is a matter of personal opinion.[53] Three of four Canadians (74 percent of adults and 80 percent of teenagers) believe that sex before marriage is all right when people love each other.[54] Even many Christians do not believe in absolute truth and believe that morality, especially sexuality, is a matter of personal preference. Many are skeptical of the authority of the Scriptures, the deity of Christ, and other central tenets of the Christian faith.[55] Churches are afraid to disciple their members into maturity or even to correct gently those who clearly transgress biblical imperatives like adultery, physical violence, or sexual abuse. Training leaders to experience the truth of the triune God is key to turning this widespread acceptance of moral relativity.

Rate yourself and the ministry in which you're involved on a scale of 1 to 4, with 1 being truth as relative and 4 being truth as absolute.		
Canadian Church Symptom	**My Rating**	**Ministry Rating**
1. All truth is relative. 2. Morality is a matter of personal preference. 3. The Bible is the final authority for faith and practice. 4. Jesus is the Truth.		

Passionate Spirituality

The Scriptures show how the early disciples went from hiding amongst themselves due to fear (Luke 24:36; John 20:19) to passionately living their lives before God. In contrast, Canadian Christians are reserved, polite, and genteel regarding spiritual matters. The early Christians experienced something so profound when they encountered the living risen Christ that they were transformed into passionate, persistent, and hopeful witnesses. The Book of Acts paints a picture of how the early disciples were all filled with boldness and spoke the Word of God fearlessly, once the Holy Spirit came upon them (Acts 4:32). Even faced with persecution (Acts 8:1), the disciples

---

53. Posterski, *Where's a Good Church*, 98.
54. Posterski and Bibby, *Emerging Generation*, 83.
55. Walsh, "Striving for Relevance in a Changing Nation," 317.

confidently "preached the word wherever they went" (8:4). As men and women with a cause, these early believers traveled around Asia Minor sharing the love of the Father, the forgiveness of the Son, and the empowerment of the Holy Spirit. They ignored threats, intimidation, prisons, beatings, even death itself (Acts 7:54–60) because they had experienced the reality of the triune God in their midst and were certain that this reality would last forever. They worked passionately as agents in God's mission, witnessed to the reality of Christ's death and resurrection, and looked forward to his second coming. The early disciples eagerly awaited and worked diligently for the restoration of all things to the original beauty and purpose for which they were designed.

Canadian Christians are reserved, dispassionate, and somewhat unemotional about spiritual truths; some even pray that Christ not return until after they have had a chance to enjoy their life here on earth. At a Christian concert in Toronto, the performers demonstrated the difference between exuberant New Yorkers and the Canadian crowd. Hoping to inspire more enthusiasm, the lead performer gave the Canadian crowd a "New York passport for the evening," thereby granting the crowd permission to "act like a New Yorker" for the night.[56] All of a sudden, the enthusiasm in the room became electric. Why do Canadian Christians need permission to get excited about the King of Kings? Why must Canadians pretend to be Americans in order to passionately express their love and devotion to the lover of their soul? The church needs leaders who will live their lives authentically and passionately for the sake of the gospel. Christ's sacrifice deserves nothing less than leaders who can ignite passionate spirituality in the Canadian church.

Rate yourself and the ministry in which you're involved on a scale of 1 to 4, with 1 being private faith and 4 being passionate spirituality.		
Canadian Church Symptom	**My Rating**	**Ministry Rating**
1. My worship is private. I don't let anyone know about it. 2. I am more reserved when I worship God. 3. I worship God passionately. 4. I worship God will all my heart, soul, mind, and strength.		

---

56. Soweto Gospel Concert, Hummingbird Centre, Toronto, February 17, 2005.

2

Belonging in Canada

One must have a notion of "belonging" in a place before any interest in engaging society emerges. Fortunately, in most provinces, except for Quebec, over 90 percent of Canadians describe their sense of belonging in Canada as very strong or somewhat strong,[1] while 75 percent of Quebec residents experience a strong sense of belonging in Canada.[2] Surprisingly, immigrants experience an even greater sense of belonging than Canadian-born citizens.[3] Yet, despite a strong sense of belonging, many are content simply to blend in with the culture rather than working toward positive transformation.

To make matters worse, Canadians often insulate themselves by practicing a type of cocooning, largely due to the harsh winters. Canadian Christians also seclude themselves by enjoying the fellowship of the saints while neglecting social issues. Many churches maintain the status quo of religious programs with no directive leadership toward a more transformative vision.[4] Instead, churches ought to be places where authentic community can be developed, a message of hope proclaimed, and a transformative force unleashed. In such an authentic community, believers can be equipped to share Christ's message of hope to an increasingly skeptical world and can make a positive impact in their families, their workplaces,

1. "2003 General Social Survey on Social Engagement."
2. Ibid.
3. Ibid.
4. Seim, interview by author.

and in the community. When developing such a community is no longer seen as optional, but as Christ's hands and feet bringing about positive and lasting transformation, skeptics will stop decrying Christianity and start considering the true claims of the gospel.

APATHY AS BLENDING IN WITH THE CULTURE

Along with Canadians' value of being tolerant is our preference for blending into the patchwork quilt of cultures around us. We prefer to live our own private, individual lives and not bother our neighbors, rather than become transformative agents of social change in our neighbourhood and our city. Sadly, by hanging such "do not disturb" signs on the doors of our lives, we not only have shut out God but also one another. The result is disconnection, loneliness, cynicism, and suspicion. These two social realities have contributed to the Canadian experience of isolation: individualism and privatization of faith.

Individualism

Canada is more than simply a country of different cultures. There are also tribes within cultures, clans within tribes, and individuals within clans. Canadians are not just a mosaic, opines Bibby, but they are "mosaics within mosaics. . . . We now have not only a cultural mosaic, but also a moral mosaic, a meaning system mosaic, a family structure mosaic, a sexual mosaic."[5] Canadians value individualism to such a degree that creating a deep sense of belonging or concern for the larger community is extremely difficult. As journalist Jonathon Gatehouse quipped: "Canada used to have an identity crisis. Now we just suffer from multiple personalities."[6]

Since Canada has elevated its Charter of Rights and Freedoms without providing a counterbalancing "Charter of Social Responsibility,"[7] Canadian society now lacks a culture of community. Instead, it displays a culture of individualism. Bibby further observes, "Individually, we have been emancipated, socially we are in disarray."[8] In previous societies, the

---

5. Bibby, *Mosaic Madness*, 9.
6. Gatehouse, "Maclean's Poll 2006," 44.
7. Bibby, *Mosaic Madness*, 13.
8. Ibid., 15.

word "individualism" did not exist, because there was no individual who did not belong to a group and who could be considered absolutely alone.[9] People are "drifting away from each other," in a process John L. Locke calls "atomization."[10] As a result, Canadians have become *solo sapiens*.[11] Today, individualism is the Canadian way of life that emphasizes individual liberty, the primacy of the individual, and the virtues of self-reliance and personal independence.

Privatization of Faith

In the past quarter century, Canadians have witnessed many scandals in organized religion. In 1989, Roman Catholic priests were found guilty of sexually and physically abusing boys at the Mount Cashel Orphanage in Newfoundland and Labrador.[12] Then, between 1994 and 1997, seventy-four people committed suicide in Quebec as part of their active membership in a religious cult called the Order of the Solar Temple.[13] Along with religious conflicts on a global scale, which are mentioned almost daily on the news, it is little wonder that Canadians have turned away from public institutions to a more private expression of religion. "Faith, like charity, seems to begin at home," comments Chris Wood. "Both may also end there."[14]

The result has been a dramatic decline in church attendance in the second half of the twentieth century. Gallup polls indicate that 65 percent of the adult population in Canada attended a religious service in 1945. Bibby recounts how that percentage slipped to 50 percent in 1950, down to 30 percent in 1970, and bottomed at 20 percent in the 1990s.[15] In the 1960s, 80 percent of Roman Catholics attended weekly church services; in the 1990s, only 30 percent did. During the 1940s, 50 percent of Protestants were weekly attendees, while today only 20 percent are. Other religions (Jewish, Hindu, Buddhist, Sikh) also are declining, from about 35 percent in the 1950s to 15 percent in the 1970s.[16] Bibby believes that this decline

9. Locke, *Devoicing of Society*, 125.
10. Ibid.
11. Ibid.
12. "Notorious Mount Cashel Orphanage to Close."
13. "Solar Temple: A Cult Gone Wrong."
14. Wood, "1988 Maclean's Decima Poll," 37.
15. Bibby, *Unknown Gods*, 4.
16. Ibid.

Part 1: The State of Leadership in the Canadian Church

finally has slowed and, in some cases, is reversing to signify a "renaissance of religion in Canada";[17] others, however, are not so optimistic.[18]

Isolation

Individualism and privatization have eroded a sense of community, leaving Canadians feeling isolated and alone. All human beings crave significant connections with others (albeit at different levels), because God has designed humanity for community (Gen 2:18). Canadians say that they desire freedom most of all with family life, being loved, and friendships being the next most coveted desires.[19] While Canadians want relationships, they also desire freedom and privacy.[20] It seems Canadians want to get close but not too close. While some believe that America is the "loneliest nation on the earth,"[21] it appears that Canadians are even more alone. This Canadian individualism presents a cold welcome to new immigrants who come from more hospitable and communal cultures. The unfortunate result is that, for most newcomers, "loneliness becomes your only friend."[22]

THE CANADIAN CHURCH: A LACK OF BELONGING

The early church provided a vastly different experience of community than the Canadian church provides for believers today. Rather than being insular, the early church transformed the surrounding community with their radical lifestyle. Instead of cocooning themselves with like-minded individuals, the early believers reached out to those who had yet to come to know the living, risen Savior. In order to win an individualistic Canadian audience, the Canadian church must become a safe environment where genuine searching and dialog can take place. As believers embrace vulnerability, brokenness, and humility, hardened hearts are softened. As Canadian Christians are genuinely hopeful in the midst of difficult or despairing circumstances, cynicism loses its grip. As the Canadian church leads in environmental concerns and

---

17. Bibby, *Restless Gods*.
18. Bowen, *Christians in a Secular World*, 14.
19. Bibby, *Boomer Factor*, 112.
20. Privacy ranks as the fifth most wanted value in 2005, according to Bibby, *Boomer Factor*, 112; see also, Bibby, *Bibby Report*, 2.
21. Frazee, *Connecting Church*, 23.
22. Garcia, "Life of a Newcomer to Canada," 17.

social justice issues, the kingdom rule and reign is proclaimed. As leaders equip believers to share the gospel respectfully, yet boldly, cynics may take another look. When church is no longer seen as optional but as central in each believer's life, the prodigals will come home.

An Authentic Community

Early believers in Christ were fiercely committed to one another in prayer, in love, and sharing life together. In contrast, many Canadian Christians feel unconnected and alone in their local churches. With God as their Father, the early church viewed themselves as God's family (Eph 2:19; 3:14). They were a community who loved and shared daily existence (1 Thess 2:8) as well as their resources (Acts 2:42–44) with one another. No one lacked anything, for all the believers shared their possessions, and they were one in heart and mind (Acts 4:32–36).

The reality in many Canadian churches is that Christians shake one another's hands but rarely know one another's names. Even if they attend services faithfully, many still lack a sense of belonging and connection to a faith community.[23] They even may volunteer on a committee or join a small group but often are left feeling no more connected than before. The Canadian church needs to develop leaders who can foster a sense of genuine community. As Frazee rightly observes, "The future of the church depends on whether it develops true community."[24]

Rate yourself and the ministry in which you're involved on a scale of 1 to 4, with 1 being more isolated and alone in your community and 4 being a sense of belonging and connection to your faith community.		
Canadian Church Symptom	**My Rating**	**Ministry Rating**
1. I feel very isolated and alone in my faith community. 2. I feel somewhat isolated and disconnected from my faith community. 3. I feel somewhat cared for and connected to others in my faith community. 4. I feel very cared for and connected to others in my faith community.		

---

23. This feeling is the strongest among young people, who often remark that they "just don't fit in."

24. Frazee, *Connecting Church*, 13.

Part 1: The State of Leadership in the Canadian Church

A Message of Hope

The Scriptures portray an extremely hopeful community of believers, even in the midst of severe persecution; by contrast, many postmodern Christians are cynical of leadership and institutions and hold a pessimistic outlook of life in general. Cynics hold "highly skeptical attitudes towards social norms" and "question the validity of popular beliefs, morality and wisdom."[25] In fact, the present age is sometimes referred to as "the age of cynicism."[26] Pessimism is a general belief that things are bad and will become worse. It is like being without hope. Such a lack of hope can be seen in the rate of suicide among young people, the second leading cause of death, after motor vehicle accidents.[27] In Canada, not only are pessimism and cynicism prevalent in the society, but also they are creeping into the church.

Paul equates being without hope as being without God (Eph 2:12). He boldly declared that if Christians' hope is only for this life, then they ought "to be pitied more than all others" (1 Cor 15:19). He prayed for the Christians in Rome that the "God of hope would fill them with all joy and peace . . . so that they would overflow with hope" (Rom 15:13). The writer to the Hebrews likened the Christian's hope to an "anchor for the soul, firm and secure" (Heb 6:19).

In contrast, there is a growing cynicism toward most leadership and institutions in Canada today. In the 1990s, Canadians indicated a "decreased confidence in leadership in just about every sphere of life."[28] Rather than the Canadian culture of loneliness and cynicism infiltrating the church, the church ought to infiltrate the culture with a message of hope and a community of grace. Unfortunately, "churches are floundering at a time when they should be flourishing."[29] Aware of this growing caution and suspicion, Christian institutions have capitalized on this by branding themselves with slogans like "the unseminary"[30] or "a church for those not into church."[31]

---

25. Todd, "B.C. [sic] Psychotherapist Tries to Make Virtue a Reality in age of Cynicism."

26. Ibid.

27. Canadian Children's Rights Council, "Reflections on Youth Suicide."

28. Bibby, *Bibby Report*, 110.

29. Bibby, *There's Got to Be More*, 8.

30. Cusick, "Conversation with Eugene Peterson."

31. Meeting House, "Some Thoughts on the Value of Religion."

The rapid growth of these two particular institutions only confirms the deep-seated skepticism that resides even in many Christians.

Rate yourself and the ministry in which you're involved on a scale of 1 to 4, with 1 being more jaded and cynical about life, people, and the future and 4 being more optimistic and hopeful about life, people, and the future.		
Canadian Church Symptom	**My Rating**	**Ministry Rating**
1. I am very skeptical. 2. I am somewhat skeptical. 3. I am somewhat optimistic. 4. I am very optimistic.		

A Transformative Force

The early church was a transformative force that turned the world upside down, whereas the Canadian church's privatized faith has exerted little or no influence on postmodern culture. The Canadian church has the potential to be a world leader in environmental concerns by alleviating poverty, fighting Acquired Immunodeficiency Syndrome (AIDS), caring for the elderly, and championing other social concerns and social justice issues. Instead, the Canadian church has been pushed to the sidelines while other influences dominate the Canadian landscape. Many Christians see no relevance between their faith and their work. Many simply do not care.

Jesus, however, saw his relationship with the Father very differently from the current climate of privatized faith. To Jesus, a relationship with the Creator affected every aspect of life and not just the personal, private realm. When Jesus proclaimed the good news of the kingdom of God, he intended for the rule and reign of God to take control of believers' hearts and lives. Not one area would be left untouched. God's rule was intended to break into human relationships, homes, workplaces, attitudes, motives, thoughts, speech, actions, decisions, finances, convictions, and social involvement.

Peter referred to believers as aliens and strangers in the world (1 Pet 2:11). He called them to be a holy nation—those who were called out, separate, and different from those around them—because they were God's chosen people (1 Pet 2:9). Throughout history, Christians have led the way in terms of concern for the poor, sick, and uneducated. In times of awakening and revival, great social changes have been made.[32] In contrast to

---

32. For example, when Charles Finney gave an altar call for people to accept Christ,

Part 1: The State of Leadership in the Canadian Church

the countercultural influence of the early church, Canadian Christians are isolated individuals whose lifestyle and values are similar to the rest of the population.

Rate yourself and the ministry in which you're involved on a scale of 1 to 4, with 1 being not very active in justice initiatives and 4 being very active in justice initiatives.		
Canadian Church Symptom	**My Rating**	**Ministry Rating**
1. I am not very active in justice initiatives. 2. I am not really active in justice initiatives. 3. I am somewhat active in justice initiatives. 4. I am very active in justice initiatives.		

Boldly Sharing One's Faith Journey

The Scriptures describe how all the believers boldly shared their faith and spoke about God's truth unashamedly after they prayed and were filled with the Holy Spirit (Acts 4:31). In contrast, many Canadian Christians are fearful of sharing their personal faith story and timid about having spiritual conversations with others. Some question the exclusive claims of Christ; others wonder if God punishes people with a different worldview. Few ever have led anyone to Christ. Most Canadians view discussing spiritual topics as socially awkward and religion as strictly taboo. When Canadian Christians experience God, they are reticent to share about their experience because they fear ridicule or alienation.

The early believers were witnesses to the resurrection and courageously shared their experience with others wherever they went. Peter and John were imprisoned by the temple guards for proclaiming that Jesus had risen from the dead (Acts 4:2). Stephen and James were martyred for their faith (Acts 7:54–60; 12:2). Paul and Barnabas were sent throughout Asia Minor by the church to proclaim the good news of Christ (Acts 13:2), and they spoke powerfully and fearlessly for the Lord (Acts 14:3). Paul, in writing to his friend Philemon, admonished him and the church in his home: "Be active in sharing your faith, so that you will have a full understanding of every good thing that we have in Christ" (Phil 1:6).

Canadian Christians, by contrast, are reserved, shy, and shrink from personally sharing their faith journey. Some feel inferior and intimidated

---

he then made them sign up to declare that either they were opposed to slavery or in favor of women suffrage. Amanatides, "Women Risking for the Kingdom."

by judgmental labels placed on them by adamant secularists. Many have bought into a false notion that religion belongs only in the sacred, private sphere. Not wanting to be labeled "fanatical," like some who use religion to perpetuate hatred and war, Christians tacitly have decided that religion is not only a private matter but also a taboo subject as well. Asking people about faith is tantamount to asking them about their sex life—it is a very intimate, sacred, and private affair that most do not share readily with strangers. Understanding this reluctance of Canadians to discuss their faith publicly is no reason for those who claim to follow Christ to do likewise. Jesus had little hesitation in announcing the kingdom of God publicly and neither did his followers. As people who have given God full sovereignty in their lives, Christians are God's ambassadors (1 Cor 5), witnesses to God's kingdom wherever they go—at home, at work, in the mall, at school, or at play.

Rate yourself and the ministry in which you're involved on a scale of 1 to 4, with 1 being more reserved in speaking about spiritual matters and 4 being a passionate witness.		
Canadian Church Symptom	**My Rating**	**Ministry Rating**
1. I am uncomfortable speaking about spiritual matters. 2. I speak about my faith only when asked. 3. I sometimes engage others in spiritual conversations. 4. I actively seek to engage others in spiritual conversations and have no hesitancy in witnessing to Christ's kingdom.		

The Church as Essential

The Scriptures describe the church as the Body of Christ (1 Cor 12), an essential and chosen instrument acting as his hands and feet in a broken and hurting world. In contrast, very few Christians see church attendance as important in their spiritual journey. In fact, many postmodern Christians question the necessity of going to church. The belief that church as optional is widely held among Canadian Christians.

As the Body of Christ, the early believers saw Christ as the head and each individual member as connected to the Head and to one another in a dynamic organism that represents God to the world. The writer of Hebrews

Part 1: The State of Leadership in the Canadian Church

exhorts Christians, "Let us not give up meeting together, as some are in the habit of doing, but let us encourage one another—and all the more as you see the Day approaching" (Heb 10:25). The implication was that "the church is not an optional afterthought . . . [but] central to God's plan of salvation."[33] The early disciples understood that God saves people into a new community and not as isolated individuals. There is no such thing as solo Christianity.

Canadian Christians, however, view the church as an optional institution and unnecessary for spiritual growth, as indicated by declining church attendance in the past fifty years.[34] While a "solid majority of Canadians continue to believe in God, the divinity of Jesus, and life after death,"[35] only 20 percent of the population attend church weekly. This optional attitude towards the church is indicative of the individualistic, "me"-centered culture. Unless there is a committed understanding of a believer's relationship with a community, people cannot experience a sense of belonging and care. Perhaps this is why many Canadians feel isolated, alone, highly cynical, and skeptical of most religious leaders and institutions.

Rate yourself and the ministry in which you're involved on a scale of 1 to 4, with 1 regarding church attendance as non-essential and 4 regarding church attendance as essential for your spiritual growth.		
Canadian Church Symptom	**My Rating**	**Ministry Rating**
1. I do not think that weekly church attendance is essential.		
2. I do not think that weekly church attendance is important.		
3. I think that weekly church attendance is important.		
4. I think that weekly church attendance is essential.		

---

33. Ogden, *Transforming Discipleship*, 32.
34. Baril and Mori, "Leaving the Fold."
35. Bibby, *Bibby Report*, 130.

3

Behaving in Canada

To lead effectively in Canada one must understand Canadian values and the sociological trends affecting Canada today. This chapter examines Canadians' top value of autonomy as an expression of the glaring symptom of apathy found throughout the country. Next, it presents a brief summary of the trends affecting Canadians. Finally, this chapter shows how these values and trends produce a lack of engagement in one's faith.

APATHY AS BEING AUTONOMOUS

According to Bibby, the number one value in Canada is personal autonomy.[1] "Canadians value their own personal freedom above everything, including family life and love."[2] Michael Adams, another Canadian sociologist, together with Amy Langstaff and David Jamieson, describes the cultural differences between Canada and the United States. He demonstrates how the founding ideas and institutions of Canada and the United States have resulted in completely unintended and unanticipated consequences. He ponders:

> Why [is it that] an initially "conservative" society like Canada has ended up producing an autonomous, inner-directed, flexible, tolerant, and socially liberal, and spiritually eclectic people while an initially "liberal" society like the United States has ended up

1. Bibby, *Boomer Factor*, 112.
2. Righton, "Maclean's Poll."

producing a people who are, relatively speaking, materialistic, outer-directed, intolerant, socially conservative, and deferential to traditional institutional authority[?][3]

He shows how a "conservative" country, founded on the values of "peace, order, and good government," produces individuals who feel secure enough to become autonomous.[4] In contrast to the stereotypical, individualistic American, his research indicates that Canadians are more autonomous, less outer-directed, and less conformist than Americans.[5]

Valuing autonomy means that Canadians are free not to care about anyone or anything. Being passive, undisciplined, or dispassionate in the public's opinion is not inappropriate or bad, but only a lifestyle option that Canadians can chose freely. No one has the right to pronounce value-laden judgments on anyone's behavior. Some even might assert boldly that it is Canadians' national right to be complacent. Bibby explains, "We value our Charter of Rights and Freedoms but take no thought about our social responsibility."[6] An examination of the current trends affecting Canadian society contributes to a deeper understanding of these "autonomous" Canadians.

TRENDS AFFECTING CANADIAN SOCIETY

The world is becoming increasingly more complex and chaotic. Canadians live with many pressures and insecurities. Families and relationships have become fractured and fragmented. Consequently, perhaps to avoid the pain of brokenness, lives are lived at expeditious velocity. Dallas Willard compares this lifestyle to "flying a high-speed aircraft upside down."[7] A number of factors contribute to the rapidly changing landscape of Canada: urbanization, mobilization, globalization, immigration, and rapid technological advance. These factors also affect the changing face of the Canadian church.

---

3. Adams with Langstaff et al., *Fire and Ice*, 10.
4. Ibid., 125.
5. Ibid., 123.
6. Bibby, *Mosaic Madness*, 13.
7. Willard, *Divine Conspiracy*, 2.

Urbanization

Canada is home to thirty-five million of the world's seven billion people.[8] It is no surprise that Canada's cities are growing; what is surprising is the rate of growth. In 1800, 5 percent of the population lived in urban areas. By 1871, that percentage grew to almost 20 percent. Fifty years later, the percentage of people living in urban centers rose to almost 50 percent of the population.[9] Today, over 80 percent of Canada's population is urbanized.[10] In Canada 62 percent of the population lives in twenty-five metropolitan areas, each with a population over one hundred thousand. A third of all Canadians live in one of the three largest cities (Toronto, Montreal, and Vancouver)—one of every six in the Greater Toronto Area.[11]

Canada's rapid urbanization has many implications for the church, since there is an inverse relationship between the size of the community and church attendance. Bibby shows that the percentage of those attending church services in smaller communities is significantly greater than those living in urban areas (31 percent attend in communities smaller than ten thousand, while 22 percent attend in communities greater than four hundred thousand).[12] People with a marginal commitment to the church in a small town often will abandon that commitment when they move to a larger city.[13] As Canada's population increasingly becomes urbanized, there will continue to be a negative impact on church attendance.

Moreover, the Canadian church is divided between rural and urban. In Brian Seim's opinion, the rural church is more active spiritually, but its members fear the city and marginalize the voice of urban Christians. Leaders in the urban church are fearful of diversity and often equate diversity with pluralism. This is true of both Francophone and Anglophone church leaders, along with other ethnic church leaders. The end result is a protectionism that often ends in the preservation of cultural characteristics rather than a full embrace of Christ's call in the lives of leaders.[14]

---

8. CBC, "Canadian Population Surpasses 35 Million."
9. Statistics Canada, "Population, Urban and Rural."
10. Kraft and Jarman, "How Current Trends," 342.
11. Ibid.
12. Bibby, *Bibby Report*, 127.
13. Walsh, "Striving for Relevance in a Changing Nation," 319.
14. Seim, interview by author.

Part 1: The State of Leadership in the Canadian Church

Mobilization

In addition to increased urbanization, Canadians are now more mobile than ever. Over 40 percent of Canadians moved between the last two censuses.[15] Approximately three of four people drive to work. More specifically, for every thirteen people going to work, ten drive, one is a passenger, one takes transit, and one walks.[16] When I was growing up (in the 1970s) we walked to church; today providing enough parking spaces is a significant challenge, especially for urban churches.

Increased mobilization means that churchgoers are more selective when it comes to choosing a worship service than they were fifty years ago, when there was only one option in town. This discerning attitude matches the Canadian consumer mentality and eclectic spirituality. Therefore, churches must satisfy parishioners' needs or find their congregants looking elsewhere.

Globalization and Immigration

In addition to other changes, the world has become smaller due to globalization and the Internet. Many businesses use the dictum "think globally, act locally" when thinking strategically about their business plan. Similarly, churches no longer can remain enclaves of the faithful few but must seek to reach out globally by starting locally. The integrity and mission of a church will be revealed by its ability to communicate in the languages, symbols, and words used by other ethnic groups. Churches need the ability to "talk to intimates in the idiom of this week and to strangers in the symbols of global understanding."[17] Since the mission of God announces Christ's kingdom to the entire world (John 3:16), Christians must be active in connecting with other nationalities using their language, idioms, and symbols.

Moreover, by the year 2016 visible minorities are projected to increase by over 250 percent in Canada, from 2.7 million in 1991 to 7.1 million in 2016.[18] In Toronto and Vancouver, minorities are quickly becoming the majority, as the population of visible minorities is estimated to increase

---

15. Statistics Canada, "Canadians on the Move."
16. Statistics Canada, "Employed Labour Force."
17. Bandy, *Coaching Change*, 116.
18. Kraft and Jarman, "How Current Trends," 345.

to 50 percent of those cities' populations by the year 2016.[19] Churches in urban centers, especially, have a great potential to reach many unreached people groups whom God conveniently is bringing to Canada's doorstep.

Rapid Technological Advance

The pace of technological change is becoming increasingly fast. Whirlwind change hurtles us at incredible speeds into the future. As a result of increased demands, Canadians' primary concern is not having enough time.[20] This affects their choice of whether or not to become involved in a faith community. Many come to the same conclusion as Bill Gates, who, when interviewed by *Time Magazine*, said, "Just in terms of allocation of time resources, religion is not very efficient. There's a lot more I could be doing on a Sunday morning."[21]

The implementation of technology also influences the values of a society by changing expectations and realities. "Technology is more than methodology: it is the way people discover and interpret meaning in life . . . about the way people discover God and interpret their experiences of the Holy."[22] For instance, the degree to which boomers valued property is the degree to which postmoderns value technology.[23] Twenty-first-century people value communication in the same way that twentieth-century people valued location.[24] Churches that do not speak in the technological language of today stop communicating the good news tomorrow.

THE CANADIAN CHURCH: A LACK OF ENGAGEMENT

A comparison between the early church and the Canadian church reveals a noticeable lack of engagement. Believers in the early church were fully surrendered and available for God. Consequently, they were fully engaged in the work of the ministry and spiritual exercises that enhanced their faith. Believers in the early church also encountered their society, turning the

---

19. Ibid.
20. Righton, "Maclean's Poll."
21. Keillor, "Faith at the Speed of Light."
22. Bandy, *Coaching Change*, 107 and 115.
23. Ibid., 116.
24. Ibid.

world upside down by their boldness and their witness. In contrast, Canadian Christians are content to sit back, relax, and enjoy God's blessings without rolling up their sleeves and fully committing themselves to the work of the ministry or the practices needed to produce genuine spiritual growth.

True Engagement

In the early church, everyone was engaged fully in the work of ministry; in the Canadian church, most passively enjoy the labors of a few. God envisioned a community of believers where each makes an important contribution to the larger community. By giving each person spiritual gifts (Eph 4:7; Rom 12:6; 1 Cor 7:7), God ensures that everyone has a unique role to play. There is no need for envy or competition, because God gives a special assignment to each member of the Body of Christ that is uniquely designed to suit individual gifts and personalities. God's anointing and favor rest on each member for that person's specific calling.

By contrast, 20 percent of church volunteers are doing 80 percent of the work. In addition, only 20 percent of the givers (statistically, the older givers)[25] contribute 80 percent of the finances. This means that many in the pew are spectators instead of active participants. Few are involved in actively engaging the surrounding community. What is lacking in the Canadian church is a clear call to genuinely engage in the mission of God. Canada needs leaders to equip and mobilize members to be active in using their gifts in service to one another and to the larger community around them.

Rate yourself and the ministry in which you're involved on a scale of 1 to 4, with 1 being a passive recipient and 4 being a proactive minister.		
Canadian Church Symptom	**My Rating**	**Ministry Rating**
1. I don't think I have any spiritual gifts. When I go to church, I am a passive observer. 2. I don't know my spiritual gifts, but I appreciate others' service at church. 3. I am learning about my spiritual gifts and I serve whenever and wherever I am able. 4. I know my gifts and I am active in regularly serving according to my gifts or wherever is most needed.		

25. Kraft and Jarman, "How Current Trends," 347–49.

Practicing Spiritual Disciplines

The Scriptures paint a picture of the early followers of Christ regularly practicing spiritual disciplines in order to grow spiritually; in contrast, Canadian Christians, while desiring to grow spiritually, are uninformed and undisciplined in their use of the disciplines for spiritual growth. Jesus modeled a lifestyle lived in complete dependence on the Father. One can rationalize that since Jesus was fully divine it was easier for him to commune with God than it is for us today. However, this argument fails to recognize that Jesus depended on the Father as a human being through the power of the Holy Spirit. As a human, Jesus knew that he could not depend on God without practicing spiritual disciplines to train his flesh to do all that God wanted it to do—including submitting to the cross. So, he practiced spiritual disciplines like Scripture reading and memorization (Luke 4:4, 8, 12), solitude (Luke 4:42), worship (Luke 4:16), fasting (Matt 6:16), and prayer (Luke 6:12). His followers also adopted a disciplined lifestyle (2 Tim 1:7), realizing that apart from God they could do nothing (John 15:1).

Paul uses the images of being an athlete, a soldier, and a farmer to paint a picture of the normal Christian life (1 Cor 9:25; 2 Tim 2:3–5). Athletes must train their muscles exceedingly hard to make them perform on the day of competition; similarly, soldiers are disciplined to win on the day of battle; and farmers, likewise, work hard to reap a crop at harvest time. Paul expects no less from those who follow Christ.

Canadian Christians, on the other hand, are quite different. When it comes to spiritual disciplines like Scripture reading and memorization, worship attendance, solitude, or fellowship designed to help stimulate spiritual growth, Canadian Christians are severely lacking. Without a focused, regular commitment to some type of spiritual exercise, it is difficult to make choices that reflect Christ's character and heartbeat. Since Canadian Christians do not regularly practice spiritual disciplines, their behavior lacks the consistency needed to make significant positive changes in their communities, workplaces, and families. Willard agrees with this example: "A baseball player who expects to excel in the game without adequate exercise of his body is no more ridiculous than the Christian who hopes to be able to act in the manner of Christ when put to the test without the appropriate exercise in godly living."[26]

---

26. Willard, *Spirit of the Disciplines*, 4–5.

Part 1: The State of Leadership in the Canadian Church

Interestingly, studies have shown that there is a direct connection between experiencing God and practicing the spiritual discipline of prayer. Of all Canadians, 47 percent say they have experienced God,[27] the same percentage as those who pray regularly (either daily or weekly).[28] Surprisingly, not many Christians recognize this correlation between other spiritual disciplines and spiritual growth. Therefore, in order for the Canadian church to grow spiritually leaders must model, teach, and motivate Canadian Christians to practice the disciplines for spiritual growth.

Rate yourself and the ministry in which you're involved on a scale of 1 to 4, with 1 being spiritually undisciplined and 4 being spiritually disciplined.		
Canadian Church Symptom	My Rating	Ministry Rating
1. I am unfamiliar with spiritual disciplines.		
2. I am familiar with spiritual disciplines, but I do not practice any on a regular basis.		
3. I regularly practice spiritual disciplines to help me grow spiritually.		
4. I have specific, measurable goals related to my spiritual development, which can only be achieved through regularly practicing spiritual disciplines.		

THE UNIMAGINABLE IMAGINED

Canada needs Christians who exhibit genuine love and true tolerance to all, including those who disagree with them. When Christians stand firm on issues of morality in gentle and loving ways, a tremendously positive impact will be made on society. Canadian Christians must make a ruthless commitment to the truth. When the Canadian church builds authentic community by sharing life and resources with one another, regardless of denominational affiliation, a strong message of hope will be proclaimed to a despairing world.

Canada needs Christians in the marketplace, in the arts, in education, in government, and every strata of society, being true to the Creator's calling and gifting in their lives. Instead of blending in, Canadian Christians must become a transformative force for good in society and must fearlessly

---

27. Bibby, *Restless Gods*, 147.

28. Ibid., 159. In 2005 this figure decreased to 45 percent, according to Bibby, *Boomer Factor*, 189.

share their faith journey with others, providing them with opportunities to respond to the good news of Jesus Christ. The Canadian church must become a place where members recognize that the Body of Christ is not optional but an essential aspect of life, where every member is aware of and fully exercising his or her spiritual gifts, and where spiritual disciplines are practiced regularly to promote spiritual growth. In the end, Canadian Christians must become more passionate about Jesus Christ than the average Canadian is about hockey.

This is the biblical standard that God has destined for Canada. Leaders are needed to move the Canadian church from its current situation to a new reality. Unless leaders are identified, equipped, and released, the Canadian church will continue to produce mediocre results. Jim Herrington, Mike Bonem, and James Harold Furr ask a provoking question for all leaders to ponder: "If we keep doing what we've been doing, we'll keep getting what we've been getting. Can you live with that?"[29]

---

29. Herrington et al., *Leading Congregational Change*, xiii.

Part 2

A Theology of the Trinitarian Leadership Dance

PART 2

4

The Trinitarian Dance as a Model for Transformational Leadership Development

Before the world existed, God was. In every transformational act, God is. For every vision that is yet to be, God is to come. There exists no better leadership model to follow than the One who existed before any other leaders, who is sovereign over history, and who ultimately will lead the entire universe forever. The vast nature of God as Trinity reflects deep insights into transformational leadership. In order to better understand the Trinitarian Dance, or *perichoresis*, one must first consider the legitimacy of the doctrine of the Trinity. The Trinity is an appropriate model for transformational leadership development because it is biblical, foundational, and knowable.

THE TRINITY IS BIBLICAL

The word "Trinity" does not appear in the biblical text but was coined by Tertullian many years after the final books of the Bible were written.[1] Yet, the Trinity dances with love throughout the pages of Scripture. Starting from creation, the reader is introduced to the Spirit of God, or the "breath of God," hovering over the waters (Gen 1:2). The Creator speaks, and all things come into being (Gen 1:3). Jesus Christ is described in the New

---

1. George, ed., *God, the Holy Trinity*, 13.

Part 2: A Theology of the Trinitarian Leadership Dance

Testament as being with God in creation and creating all things (John 1:1–3; Col 1:16). In the final act of history, humanity will be judged by One on a great white throne (Rev 20:11). The Lamb of God, Jesus Christ, also reigns together with the One seated on this throne (Rev 22:1, 3). In addition, the Holy Spirit, who unveiled the Revelation to the Apostle John while he was in the Spirit (Rev. 1:10), is present at the end of the age and invites everyone who is thirsty to come and join the wedding feast of the Lamb (Rev 22:17). Throughout the whole testimony of Scripture, the Godhead—three in one—is revealed, often in a triune pattern (Matt 28:19; Luke 1:35; Acts 20:28; 2 Cor 13:14; Eph 1:1–14; Titus 3:4–6; Rev 1:4–5).

A legitimate concern, however, with much of the contemporary trinitarian dialog in the past seventy-five years is that it seems to be devoid of scriptural backing. Alister McGrath writes, "Much trinitarian reflection has lost its moorings in Scripture."[2] Nonetheless, Gerald L. Bray purports that in one of the earliest and most authentic books of the New Testament, the Letter to the Galatians, Paul presents the seeds for the understanding of the doctrine of the Holy Trinity that the church embraces today. "In Gal 4:6," explains Bray, "the apostle Paul lays the groundwork for his assertion about the persons of the Trinity."[3] As sons and daughters who cried, "Abba! Father!" the early Christians clearly experienced God as Father. Their experience of sonship verified God's existence as Father. They also experienced the reality and presence of the living, risen Son of God along with the presence of the Holy Spirit in their midst.[4] Consequently, God as Father, God as Spirit, and God as Son are the three characteristic ways that the early Christians experienced God, such that the Jews came to regard the Christian experience of God as incompatible with their belief in the "undifferentiated One."[5] Therefore, the Trinity, while not a biblical term, is revealed throughout the Bible. The Scriptures clearly point to one God in three persons, as described by the early church fathers in the Councils of Nicea and Constantinople.[6]

---

2. McGrath, "Doctrine of the Trinity," 26.

3. Bray, "Out of the Box," 46.

4. Ibid., 42. Bray admits that while it is not very clear whether the "spirit of his Son" refers to the Holy Spirit or is simply a rhetorical device to refer to the Son himself, the "spirit of his Son" performs the same activities as the Comforter described in John 14–16. He deduces that the "other Comforter" of John's Gospel must, therefore, be the same Holy Spirit whom Paul mentions in Galatians 4:6.

5. Ibid.

6. Kärkkäinen, *Trinity*, 31–42.

The Trinitarian Dance as a Model

THE TRINITY IS FOUNDATIONAL

The Trinity is theologically central to Christianity. An accurate comprehension of the Trinity is akin to knowing the grammatical rules of English.[7] It is as essential as bones are to the body.[8] In fact, Thomas F. Torrance believes that the doctrine of the Trinity should have primacy over all other doctrines. He writes, "It is the nerve and centre of them all," informing and integrating every other doctrine.[9] While McGrath expresses concern over whether the doctrine of the Trinity can play a foundational role in theology when it is something inferred from other foundations,[10] in my view, without the Trinity Christianity collapses. Consequently, when thinking about Christian leadership development, the Trinity supplies a foundational structuring motif.

Trinitarian thinking and writing formed the cornerstone of the early church. The idea of God as Father, Son, and Spirit could not be avoided by the early Christians when they reflected on their experience of the risen Christ, their commitment to the confession of one God, and their fellowship with the presence of the Holy Spirit among them.[11] Both the Apostles' Creed and the Nicene Creed reflect this thinking, as they are each are divided into three articles corresponding to the three persons of the Trinity. Throughout most of church history, except for a brief hiatus during the Enlightenment period, theologians have structured theology in a trinitarian pattern.[12] Confession of the triune God is the *sine qua non* of the Christian faith.[13] As such, it provides a foundation for the development of all other doctrines and praxis.[14]

An understanding of the nature of the Trinity is foundational in the sense that it describes both the "inner life" of God as well as the "external salvific work" of God. These two aspects, the inner life and the external work, represent the "eternal" and "temporal" nature of God and often are

---

7. Edgar, *Message of the Trinity*, 24.
8. Ibid.
9. Torrance, *Christian Doctrine of God*, 31.
10. McGrath, "Doctrine of the Trinity."
11. Grenz and Franke, *Beyond Foundationalism*, 173–74.
12. Ibid., 177–86. This hiatus in the eighteenth and nineteenth centuries perhaps motivated the British Council of Churches in 1989 to commission a report on trinitarian doctrine today, entitled "The Forgotten Trinity."
13. Grenz and Franke, *Beyond Foundationalism*, 170.
14. Packer, *Knowing God*, 16.

referred to as the "essential" and the "economic" aspects of the Trinity.[15] Similarly, leadership consists of the inner life and the outer work of the leader. One cannot perform great acts of leadership without having inner character and credibility. One's mind, heart, and hands must work in congruence in order to accomplish any act of leadership. In fact, it is the very transgression of this integrity that maligns leadership. A trinitarian leadership model offers a way to guide the development of truly Christian leaders.

In addition, Ray Sherman Anderson shows that the Trinity is foundational to practical theology. He argues that for a theology to be "effective in mission" it also must be "trinitarian in nature."[16] He explains how Paul, more than any other witness to the resurrection, developed a trinitarian theology as he endeavored to carry out the commission of the risen Christ in the power of the Holy Spirit. By proclaiming the gospel of Christ, he experienced the transforming power of the Holy Spirit at work in the lives of those coming to faith. Needing to remain faithful to the Law and the Prophets that declare God is one, Paul wrestled with his understanding of the relationship among the Father, the resurrected Messiah, and the Holy Spirit. In the end, "Paul argues passionately and profoundly for the unity of God in his work as Spirit within us, Christ with us, and the Father around us."[17] Anderson concludes that "practical theology is grounded in the intratrinitarian ministry of the Father toward the world, the Son's ministry to the Father on behalf of the world, and the Spirit's empowering of the disciples for ministry."[18]

THE TRINITY IS KNOWABLE

Not only is the Trinity biblical and foundational for building a model of Christian leadership; despite his ineffable nature, the Trinity is also knowable. He is knowable because, as Karl Barth has pointed out, God has made himself known to us.[19] By this self-revelation one can know God in a relational sense. The Trinity is knowable despite the paradoxical nature of "Three in One," since the doctrine of the Trinity is understandable and makes sense. Granted, there is still mystery to the Godhead, because humans

15. Edgar, *Message of the Trinity*, 24.
16. Anderson, *Shape of Practical Theology*, 39.
17. Ibid.
18. Ibid., 40.
19. Barth, *Doctrine of the Word of God*, 1:339–83.

are not God. However, mystery does not necessitate absurdity, irrationality, or illogicality.[20] The Trinity is not—as some have alleged—incomprehensible, irrelevant, or unnecessary.[21] Brian Edgar and Derek Tidball agree: "We can conceive of an idea, even if we cannot fully imagine what it means. The concept of Trinity is logical, but logic alone cannot comprehend the vastness of God."[22] Experiencing one God as Father, Son, and Holy Spirit, then, makes sense and enables ordinary believers to know God relationally and tangibly in their everyday lives.

The concept of the Trinity preserves three basic truths: "There is one and only one God, God 'subsists' in three distinct persons, and the three persons are equally divine in essence and attributes."[23] These three truths are essential to any orthodox understanding of the Trinity. Worshipping one God in three persons who are equally divine presents the God who revealed himself to the early Christians as Father, Son, and Holy Spirit. These truths are portrayed in the "shield of the Trinity," shown below in figure 1.[24]

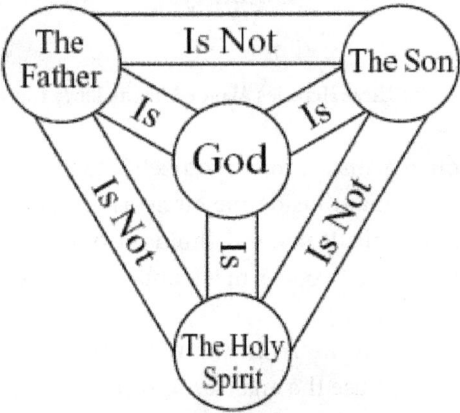

Figure 1. Shield of the Trinity

20. Johnson, *Experiencing the Trinity*, 40.

21. Theological dictionaries and seminary textbooks simply state that the Trinity is a mystery or incomprehensible. See *The New International Dictionary of the Bible: Pictorial Edition*, s.v. "Trinity." Erikson, *Christian Theology*, 338. In addition, Dorothy Sayers, in her characterization of the average churchgoer's view of the Trinity, writes, "Q: 'What is the doctrine of the trinity?' A: 'The Father incomprehensible, the Son incomprehensible, and the whole thing incomprehensible.' Something put in by theologians to make it more difficult—nothing to do with daily life or ethics." Sayers, *Whimsical Christian*, 25.

22. Edgar, *Message of the Trinity*, 21–22.

23. Johnson, *Experiencing the Trinity*, 40.

24. Ibid., 46.

Part 2: A Theology of the Trinitarian Leadership Dance

Paul D. K. Jewett states, "The church did not formulate the doctrine of the Trinity in order to resolve the mystery of God's self-revelation, but rather to preserve that mystery."[25] God has revealed himself in such a way so ordinary people can know him and enter into a relationship with him through Jesus Christ.

Figure 2 below illustrates three heresies that the early church tried to avoid.[26] Each heresy comes from holding only two of the above truths while denying the third.

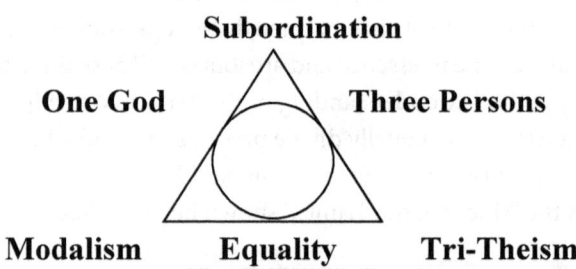

Figure 2. Three Heresies Avoided by the Early Church[27]

Darrell W. Johnson explains, "Project yourself into the center of the triangle and circle. You will remain inside the circle as long as you hold on to all three sides of the triangle. If you only hold on to two sides, you will slide into the corner where the two legs meet, and will find yourself outside the circle."[28]

Analogies help make the Trinity knowable to average believers. When explaining the Trinity, I use the analogy of someone simultaneously being a wife, daughter, and mother—three relationships of one person.[29] Saint Patrick used the analogy of a three-petalled clover.[30] Saint Augustine used

---

25. Jewett, *God, Creation, and Revelation*, 273.

26. Nicole, *Meaning of the Trinity*, 389–96.

27. This diagram is borrowed from *Standing Forth: Collected Writings of Roger Nicole*, published under the Mentor imprint of Christian Focus Publications, and is used with their kind permission.

28. Nicole, *Standing Forth*, 42.

29. Edgar critiques the relational analogy stating that humans are not like Father, Son, and Spirit, who interact and relate together. Edgar, *Message of the Trinity*, 21–22.

30. All of analogies are deficient in some way. See Erickson, *Making Sense of the Trinity*, 60–62; and Johnson, *Experiencing the Trinity*, 44.

The Trinitarian Dance as a Model

the idea of God being the Lover, the Beloved, and the Love shared among them.[31] Barth conceived of God as the Revealer, the Revelation, and the Revealedness.[32] Robert W. Jenson argues that "Father, Son, and Holy Spirit" together form a proper name for God, similar to people with a first, middle, and last name.[33] The early church fathers referred to the Holy Spirit and the Word as the two hands of God.[34] Interestingly, young believers—even young children, when given an analogy—experience little difficulty grasping the concept of one God in three persons, because they grasp it by faith. The simplicity of an analogy of three persons eternally enjoying one dance of love together does not encompass the vast philosophical and metaphysical divine mystery of the universe, but it does make it easier to personally encounter and relate to that mystery.

Sadly, analogies are inadequate and can be heretical, usually supporting some form of modalism of tritheism. Johnson explains:

> The frustration we have in finding analogies simply reminds us that the Trinitarian nature of God is not something for which there are adequate analogies. The Trinitarian nature cannot be deduced from nature. Rather it is something which can only be revealed from outside our experience. The doctrine of the Trinity is grounded not in nature but in God's self-revelation.[35]

For this reason, neither analogies nor explanations can be interchanged for a personal encounter with God as Father, Son, and Holy Spirit. Therefore, the best way to know the Trinity is by entering into a relationship with the Father, Son, and Holy Spirit and participating in the dance of love together with the triune God of grace.

Visualizing the Trinity Using a Dance Motif

Contemporary authors have described the Trinity in terms of a dance. Most notable is C. S. Lewis, who referred to God as "a kind of dance." He wrote

---

31. "Love is of someone that loves, and *with* love something *is* loved. Behold, then, there are three things: he that loves, that which is loved, and love." Augustine, *On the Holy Trinity*, 8.10.14.
32. Barth, *Doctrine of the Word of God*, 1:344.
33. Jenson, *Triune Identity*.
34. Compton, "Theophilus of Antioch and the 'Two Hands of God.'"
35. Johnson, *Experiencing the Trinity*, 45.

that one of the most important differences between Christianity and all other religions is this:

> In Christianity, God is not a static thing—not even a person—but a dynamic, pulsating activity, a life, almost a kind of drama. Almost, if you will not think me irreverent, a kind of dance. . . . The whole dance, or drama, or pattern of this three-Personal life is to be played out in each one of us . . . each one of us has got to enter that pattern, take his place in that dance. There is no other way to the happiness for which we were made.[36]

Others have also picked up on this dance imagery when describing the Trinity. Eugene Peterson encourages his seminary students to imagine the Trinity like a "three-sided square dance."[37] The imagery, of course, begs a fourth side: humanity is invited to join in the dance with the blessed Trinity. Even Leonard Sweet, who claims he can only step an "elephantine square dance," teaches believers how to dance the "soul salsa" of life with God.[38] He remarks, "Even if I cannot dance with my feet, my 'heart can dance at the sound of His Name.' My soul can learn the dance steps of the Lord of the Dance."[39]

I imagine the Trinity as a father who picks up his jubilant children upon his arrival home after work and spins them around and around and around. I picture the joy and laughter of the child and the delight of the father watching his children enjoying his presence. Leaders must become like little children in order to enter the kingdom (Matt 18:3). The Father, Son, and Holy Spirit always are dancing with joy over Christian leaders, not due to what they accomplish for him, but simply because they are his beloved children in whom is all his delight. In fact, spiritual truths are revealed to those with childlike faith (Matt 11:25–26). Dancing with God in this Trinitarian Dance will reveal certain steps and rhythms that captivate, motivate, and transform.

The biblical certainty of the Trinity is essential for developing Christian leaders, so they can navigate a culture confidently with no fixed anchors. Historically, it has stood the test of time. Solid grounding in this foundational truth gives leaders credibility to chart the course through an uncertain future. Practically, the Trinity makes sense and makes a difference

---

36. Lewis, *Mere Christianity*, 136–37.
37. Crabb, "God's Square Dance."
38. Sweet, *Soul Salsa*, 13.
39. Ibid.

to leadership that is needed to awaken the complacent in Canada to witness to Christ's kingdom. Since the Trinity is so knowable, foundational, and biblical, it is imperative to explore further this wonderful, awesome, and beautiful reality by examining what is meant by the Trinitarian Dance, known as *perichoresis*.

THE TRINITARIAN DANCE: PERICHORESIS

The idea of *perichoresis* was implied in the fourth-century writings of the Cappadocian Fathers as they refuted the heresy of tritheism; yet the actual term *perichoresis*, with reference to the Trinity, originates from Pseudo-Cyril in the sixth century[40] and was developed more thoroughly by John of Damascus in the eighth century.[41] It comes from two Greek words: *peri*, meaning "around," and *choreo*, meaning "to penetrate, to fill or to contain." *Perichoresis* means mutual indwelling, interpenetration, coinherence, and interdependence. Erikson defines *perichoresis* as "the interpenetration of life and personality within the Godhead. [It is] the idea that the Father, Son, and Holy Spirit are bound together in such a close unity that the life of each flows through each of the others, and each has access to the thought and experience of other."[42] *Perichoresis* suggests unity, for each member of the Trinity lives fully in the life of the other. Paul S. Fiddes describes *perichoresis* as "the permeation of each person by the other, their co-inherence without confusion."[43] God the Father, Son, and Holy Spirit mutually indwell, penetrate, and depend on one another for life, yet remain distinct from each other. Catherine Mowry LaCugna explains:

> *Perichoresis* expressed the idea that the three divine persons mutually inhere in one another, draw life from one another, "are" what they are by relation to one another. . . . Each divine person is irresistibly drawn to the other, taking his/her existence from the other containing the other in him/herself, while at the same time pouring self out into the other. . . . There is no blurring of the individuality of each person, there is also no separation. There is

---

40. Pseudo-Cyril, *De Sacrosancta Trinitate*, 24.
41. John of Damascus, *Exposition of the Orthodox Faith*, 1.14.
42. Erikson, *Making Sense of the Trinity*, 57.
43. Fiddes, *Participating in God*, 71.

> only the communion of love in which each person comes to be . . . what he/she is, entirely with reference to the other.[44]

Perichoresis is an important aspect of the triune God that offers a significant contribution to developing a paradigm for transformational leadership.

Later, the idea of interpenetration came to suggest a dance motif. Translating *perichoresis* from Greek into Latin generates two meanings: *circuminsessio*, which means "to sit around," and *circumincesso*, which means "to move around." One is static, while the other is more dynamic and active—like a dance.[45] LaCugna prefers the image of a divine dance for it suggests, in her opinion, an interesting play on words: the Greek *perichoreuo*, which means "to dance around," closely resembles *perichoreo*, which means "to encircle or encompass."[46] The dance imagery conveys dynamic and creative energy: "the eternal and perpetual movement, the mutual and reciprocal permeation of each person with and in and through and by the other persons."[47] It connotes partnership in movement—"one fluid motion of encircling, encompassing, permeating, enveloping, outstretching [sic]."[48] It forbids thinking of God as solitary. So, one might rightly conceive of the Trinity as a circle dance of three persons who tango so intimately and intricately that they seem as one to onlookers.

This metaphor of a divine dance was used in the Middle Ages to describe the inner participation of God. Fiddes describes the image of a divine dance, stating, "In this dance the partners not only encircle each other and weave in and out between each other as in human dancing; in the divine dance, so intimate is the communion that they move in and through each other so that the pattern is all-inclusive."[49] This divine dance, according to Fiddes, is not so much about the dancers but about the patterns of the dance itself.[50] The patterns of the dance overlap and intersect. The dancers interweave with and through one another, whereas human dancers can only encircle around one another.

The East and West envision the divine dance slightly differently. In the Eastern church, the Father is the origin (*arche*) or the fountainhead of

44. LaCugna, *God for Us*, 270–71.
45. Ibid., 272.
46. Ibid.
47. Ibid., 271.
48. Ibid., 272.
49. Fiddes, *Participating in God*, 72.
50. Ibid.

the persons in God. The Father sends out the Son and then sends the Holy Spirit through the Son, but the Father is the originator and cause of both of the others. In this sense, there is a "progressive dance in which participants move outside the inner circle of dancers to make contact with others, and then come back again, bringing other dancers with them."[51] In contrast, the Western picture of the Trinity's communion is more like a circle dance where there is equality, mutuality, and reciprocity of the three persons.[52]

The metaphor of a dance, however, did not take hold in Christian thought, possibly due to a Platonic understanding of God as perfect and unmoving.[53] Although the early Christians did envision God as the still point of the dance, they could not conceive of a God in movement. Dance, however, implies movement and change. It is precisely this dynamic image of God that is needed to construct a model of leadership development that is flexible, active, responsive to feedback, and adjusting to change. Moreover, *the Trinitarian Dance* or *perichoresis* is extremely practical and relevant for the practice of Christian leadership in a postmodern country like Canada.

Perichoresis Makes a Difference

A trinitarian understanding of ministry is essential, because it frees pastors from debilitating stress and restores joy and delight in ministry. It is a model that acknowledges and cooperates with the Trinity's sovereign plan in the making of leaders. Roderick Leupp expands on this idea: "The Trinity is an eminently practical doctrine, not for the sake of practicality alone, but because the triune God is the living God who invites all of creation into the abundance of his life."[54] *Perichoresis* is particularly relevant to Canadian Christian leadership development, because it reduces activism, addresses unique issues in the Canadian context, and counteracts pragmatism in ministry.

---

51. Ibid., 75.
52. Ibid., 77.
53. Ibid., 73–74.
54. Leupp, *Knowing the Name of God*, 25.

Part 2: A Theology of the Trinitarian Leadership Dance

Perichoresis Reduces Activism

A trinitarian understanding of leadership provides a remedy for clergy and volunteer burnout, so rampant in the church today. Unfortunately, most Christians are "unitarian" in their understanding of God.[55] Johnson claims, "Most believers are unitarian in practice. Some are binitarian. Few are truly and fully trinitarian."[56] For instance, Christian service often is understood as something that people do for God. Understood in this way, the responsibility of Christian leaders is to envision, shape values, plan strategies, create goals, align systems, and evaluate outcomes. Leadership, then, becomes a service one does before God. This human-centered understanding reduces the high call of Christian leadership from a gift to mere work. It is unitarian because the leaders are on one side, offering their service to God, who is on the other side—hearing their visions, receiving their strategies, and judging their results.

Trinitarian leadership, on the other hand, is the gift of participating with what God is doing already in the congregation and in the community. It is receiving God's vision, allowing the life of Christ to shape one's character and corporate culture, and surrendering to the Holy Spirit's guidance. Rather than facing strict judgment for one's efforts, trinitarian leaders are assured that God is at work accomplishing his plan, sometimes despite appearances. Rather than focusing on what one can do for God, the emphasis is on the life and work of the blessed Trinity in and through the Body of Christ.

The unitarian way of leadership results in great weariness, while trinitarian leadership results in abundance of joy. It is initiated by what God already is doing, empowered by the Holy Spirit, and emphasizes living in Christ before leading others to Christ. Graham Buxton emphasizes this paradigm shift: "Caught up into the life of the triune God, we experience his grace in the steps of the dance—here there is neither striving nor weariness, for the dance is God's dance, not ours."[57] Rather than being a servant of the world on behalf of God, Christian leaders need to enter into "the ministry of Jesus to the Father, through the power of the Holy Spirit, on

---

55. "Despite their orthodox confession of the Trinity, Christians are, in their practical life, almost mere 'monotheists,'" claims Rahner, *Trinity*, 10.

56. Johnson, *Experiencing the Trinity*, 53.

57. Buxton, *Dancing in the Dark*, 301.

behalf of the world."[58] In this way, they will discover the antidote to activism and be cured of their "theological anemia."[59]

Perichoresis Addresses Issues in the Canadian Church

Perichoresis provides a remedy to what is lacking in the Canadian church. In a tolerant society that is intolerant toward Christianity, *perichoresis* presents an understanding of a God who values not only unity and harmony but also diversity and particularity. Buxton contends, "The richness of the language of *perichoresis* with respect to human community lies not only in the mutuality and reciprocity of giving and receiving, but also in its insistence that particularity is not diminished, but rather enhanced."[60] Each member of the Godhead fully accepts, embraces, and delights in the others with a mutual self-giving love. There are three distinct persons—the Father, Son, and Holy Spirit—who are not absorbed into one another, yet remain as one God. *Perichoresis* demonstrates how to be truly tolerant toward those who are distinct from oneself and how to accept plurality without embracing pluralism. Since there are three distinct entities in the Godhead, Canadians can be tolerant towards diversity in their culture. Since the Father, Son, and Holy Spirit all are united in one truth—in fact, they define truth—Canadians should not embrace relativism; rather, they should debate and evaluate the truth claims in each culture and religion to determine if statements and assertions are legitimate and contribute to the overall welfare of society.

Moreover, the Canadian culture is a sea of pluralistic, relativistic, and secularist ideas. The perichoretic Trinity, however, reveals ultimate truth in relationship. John D. Zizioulas argues that the Trinity demonstrates that truth is an eminently communal occurrence and knowledge is the outcome of communion.[61] In his opinion, the precedence of personhood over being fundamentally alters the concept of truth. Miroslav Volf explains, "Truth is no longer a certain cognitive relation between intellect and being, but rather an event of love between persons; being in truth means being in communion."[62] For a culture searching for truth in relationships, *perichoresis* provides a model of a God who is truth in relationship.

58. Anderson, *Shape of Practical Theology*, 40–46.
59. Ibid.
60. Buxton, "On the Trinitarian Doctrine of *Perichoresis*," 12–13.
61. Zizioulas, *Being as Communion*, 72–101.
62. Volf, *After Our Likeness*, 93.

Part 2: A Theology of the Trinitarian Leadership Dance

Furthermore, individualistic Canadians need a picture of community, which *perichoresis* portrays. The Father is only Father in relationship to the Son. As such, the Trinity portrays an attractive image of authentic community to a culture that is largely privatized and alone. Within the life of the Trinity there is unity and diversity, interdependence, deference, and joy. Relationships are valued more than position, and each member is given real dignity and value. Similarly, as an "icon of the Trinity,"[63] the church ought to reflect oneness, particularity, sharing of life together, mutuality, and delight. Relationships are to be treasured more than prestige or position, with each member given real dignity and value. Humans will recognize their need for one another, because they are created for relationships and only can realize their full humanity in communion with God and others. Leupp contends, "God's perfectly perichoretic life is a prescription for how people ought to live."[64] Once the Canadian church understands and starts to model the communal love displayed by perichoretic community, the lost will pay attention and want to come home to God.

Additionally, since cynicism and distrust for authority have crept into the Canadian church, *perichoresis* provides a hopeful paradigm for the local church. The radical coequality found with the Trinity provides a practical model for structuring the local church.[65] Since the Trinity's vision for community formation rejects every conceivable form of subordination, patriarchy, and hierarchy, churches that affirm equality, mutuality, cooperation, and participation will appeal greatly to a postmodern anti-authoritarian environment. Buxton says, "The more the church advocates and cultivates co-operative, rather than competitive or hierarchical ministries, the more it reflects the shared trinitarian life of co-existence in diversity."[66] Buxton refutes former Cardinal Joseph Ratzinger's hierarchical ecclesiology[67] on the basis of a perichoretic understanding of the Godhead,[68] and insists, along with Leonardo Boff, that the church become "more communion than hierarchy, more service that power, more circular than pyramidal, more

---

63. LaCugna, *God for Us*, 402.

64. Leupp, *Knowing the Name of God*, 165.

65. Buxton, *Trinity, Creation and Pastoral Ministry*, 153–66. Here Buxton refers to this as community formation and develops this idea more in depth.

66. Ibid., 157.

67. Ratzinger, *Church, Ecumenism, and Politics*, 29–62.

68. Buxton, *Trinity, Creation, and Pastoral Ministry*, 154–56.

loving embrace than bending the knee before authority."[69] As such, *perichoresis* provides a standard against which one can measure the local church. LaCugna explains, "Very simply we may ask whether our institutions, rituals, and administrative practices foster elitism, discrimination, competition, or any of several 'archisms,' or whether the church is run like God's household: a domain of inclusiveness, interdependence, and cooperation, structured according to the model of *perichoresis* among persons."[70]

Another important issue that *perichoresis* addresses is the Canadian culture of privatized faith. *Perichoresis* reveals that faith is discovered in relationship with one another, and this relationship is not insular. It is an *ekstatic* or self-giving type of relationship, which transforms the world. Transformation is, in fact, the *missio Dei* into which Christians are invited to participate. Transformation cannot be accomplished through programs; it only occurs through participation in the creative ministry of the Holy Spirit, "who choreographs the steps of all who are called into costly identification with the hurting world."[71] In order to become more transformational, Christians must be drawn from their selfish orientations into the very life of the Trinity. Mission becomes participation in the continuous creation of God[72] and seeks not just to win the lost but also to restore wholeness and balance to all of creation. By joining the Trinity in this mission, Christians become a transformational force as they witness to and participate in God's kingdom here on earth.

Furthermore, Canadians are timid people by nature and prefer not to stand out publicly. Some, not wanting to draw attention to themselves, refuse to give public testimony of their faith. The persons of the three-in-one God are not timid, however, when glorifying the other members. The Spirit seeks to glorify the Father and the Son. The Father glorifies the Son, and the Son strives to glorify the Father. This mutual deference provides a welcome alternative to Canadian Christians' shyness over sharing their faith story. Canadian Christians need to reimage witnessing as not bragging about themselves but bragging about the Trinity. While the members of the Trinity enjoy a very intimate and personal relationship with one another, they open their circle of relations to include others. Similarly, while a relationship with God is indeed personal, Canadian Christians must follow

---

69. Boff, *Trinity and Society*, 154.
70. LaCugna, *God for Us*, 402.
71. Buxton, *Dancing in the Dark*, 153.
72. Ibid., 165.

the Trinity's lead and eschew a privatized faith to unlock their faith stories to others and to include others in the dance.

Next, *perichoresis* presents a model where every member is engaged fully in the work of the ministry. The Father and the Spirit are not absent from Christ when Jesus performs his work of atonement on the cross; they are ever present together with the Son, even though he cries out in agony, "My God, my God, why have you forsaken me?" (Mark 15:34). Leupp argues, "In the cross we meet not one-third of the Trinity (if it is even possible to divide the Trinity), not Jesus acting alone, but the fullness of God."[73] Contrary to what contemporary hymn writers suggest, the Father does not turn his face away from the Son as he dies in excruciating agony.[74] How can he? In his perichoretic union with the Son, the Father not only watches the Son with intense concern but perhaps locks eyes with the Son to communicate his joint-suffering with him.[75] This is what is meant by the vulnerability of God who suffers together with those who suffer.[76] Just as all members of the Trinity are fully engaged in the work, every member of the community is given spiritual gifts by the Holy Spirit and is expected to be engaged fully in using those gifts to build up the Body of Christ. There is no competition within a perichoretic vision of God; likewise, there need not be any rivalry within the Body of Christ. Participating in God's dance, Canadian Christians will become truly engaged to make a difference in the local community and around the world.

While Canadians value their freedom more than anything else, another crucial act that *perichoresis* accomplishes is that it helps Canadian Christians realize that they are not autonomous individuals; their actions affect others in the faith community, whether they recognize it or not. When the church fathers coined the word *hypostasis*, which is translated "person," to describe the triune God in three persons, they meant a "distinct identity" that only makes sense in relationship. However, "person" today means an otherness that is alone, "a naked individuality of the mind closed in on itself."[77] The

73. Leupp, *Knowing the Name of God*, 114.
74. Townend, *How Deep the Father's Love for Us*.
75. Buxton, "Participating in the Ministry of Christ."
76. Fiddes, *Participating in God*, 170–79, expands this idea and points out that suffering must involve being changed by something or someone outside oneself or "open to being wounded." Many of the Church fathers in the middle ages refuted this notion of divine passibility, considering it heretical. Instead, they qualified God's vulnerability saying that God does not suffer or change "in exactly the small way as we do."
77. Fiddes, *Participating in God*, 6.

Canadian church must reclaim personhood as "being in communion," as Zizioulas describes.[78] Once Christians recognize their interdependence, then non-discipleship will no longer an option. Consciously choosing non-discipleship over discipleship has disastrous consequences—not only for one's own spiritual journey but also for others in the community who might look to them for inspiration. Consequently, Canadian Christians will want to learn and practice the spiritual disciplines, because they have chosen to be apprenticed to Christ and desire to do all things as he would. This desire for discipleship will not happen in an autonomous culture but will only occur when the paradigm shifts so that Canadian Christians recognize their interdependence in the community of faith.

Finally, a perichoretic vision of God presents the three persons as intensely passionate in their love for one another and in their longing for humans to be reconciled to God. This contrasts with the dispassionate Canadian church, which, as has been shown, can be apathetic and unemotional in its relationship with God. Buxton describes the Trinity's intense passion in this way: "All three rejoice not only in each other as they celebrate the divine life within the Godhead, but also in the homecoming of all who, like the wayward son in the parable in Luke 15, realize how lost they really are and who seek a place back in the family home."[79] Such a fellowship of love and emotion is overwhelming. Lovers who are caught up in joyous delight in each other reflect this type of love. Each member of the Trinity "delights in the loving relationships in the divine dance and exults in the self-emptying love."[80] God's passion is to see all of humanity forever caught up in the joy of divine love. It is a passion in which the Canadian church is invited to participate, "dancing with God in a world that has lost its way."[81]

Perichoresis Counteracts Pragmatism

The Trinitarian Dance as a model for leadership development makes a difference to the praxis of ministry because it counteracts the drift towards pragmatism. Churches inevitably have more ministry needs than volunteers to fill those needs: Sunday school ministries need Sunday school teachers, small group ministries require small group leaders, worship teams lack

78. Zizioulas, *Being as Communion*. The entire book addresses the concept in detail.
79. Buxton, *Dancing in the Dark*, 19.
80. Pinnock, *Flame of Love*, 39.
81. Buxton, *Dancing in the Dark*, 20.

worship leaders, evangelistic teams search for evangelistic leaders, and the list could go on. The Trinitarian Dance offers Canadian leaders a paradigm to train and equip others with the principles and practices of leadership. Instead of hastily mismatching people, positions, and spiritual gifts, emerging leaders will grow in their self-understanding and self-awareness. *Perichoresis* presents a robust theology of the Trinity, which contributes to a healthy model for leadership development. It is a model that produces integration and wholeness in the leaders being developed and acknowledges the Trinity's presence and power in all leadership development.

FATHER, SON, AND HOLY SPIRIT: A WARM-UP

My first experience giving an evangelistic message was at a Chinese youth event in Toronto. I focused on three essential aspects of the Trinity that are vitally important: the love of the Father, the worth of the Son, and the empowerment of the Holy Spirit. These three attributes address the basic human needs for belonging, security, and significance.[82] These truths reclaim what was lost in the fall, for they declare humanity as lovable, valuable, and capable. These essential features of the Trinity not only shaped my initial foray into evangelistic preaching but also form the initial steps needed in any leadership development—the warm-up exercise before anyone can learn to dance. As a result of that invitation, five young people came forward and dedicated their lives to God. Today, they are actively serving in their local church.

The Love of the Father

In the Garden of Eden, Adam and Eve enjoyed intimate fellowship with their Creator and with each other. They experienced total acceptance and had nothing to hide (Gen 2:25). After the fall, they were alienated from God and each other. Belonging, which was intended to be an attribute of humanity in creation, became a glaring need after the fall.[83] Acceptance was replaced by rejection, so those who come to God hunger to be completely embraced by the Father's love.

---

82. Anderson, *Victory Over the Darkness*, 31.
83. Ibid., 36.

The Trinitarian Dance as a Model

The Father loves his children unconditionally—not because they believe correctly or act appropriately, but simply because he created each one uniquely and specially in his eyes. Sadly, many never have experienced this type of unconditional love from their earthly parents. Consequently, it is hard to receive such love from their heavenly Father. As a result, many in leadership have unmet intimacy needs that only can be satisfied by being embraced by the loving heavenly Father. Sadly, many who are unable to be intimate with the Father end up being inappropriately intimate with others. This explains the large numbers of pastors who fall due to sexual immorality.[84]

The Father's love not only meets the need for belonging but also reminds humanity of its identity as divine image-bearers. C. Baxter Kruger elaborates:

> Our great problem as human beings is not that we have been left out of the circle; our great problem is that we have no idea who we are and what has become of us in Jesus Christ. We have been duped, deceived about Jesus and about ourselves. We have been sold a bill of goods, lied to, confused. We have underestimated Jesus Christ. And as a result, we have misjudged who we are and what is actually happening in our ordinary lives.[85]

When this happens, the evil one whispers the "we are nots": we are not special, not acceptable, not good enough, not included, and not beautiful.[86] This lie forms a "lethal roux" of insecurity, anxiety, and fear which drives humanity to search for fullness in everything else. In a frantic search for a solution to the emptiness, many become "human vacuum cleaners in our neediness."[87] To discover the truth about the Father and the truth about one's identity in him is to have a "different roux" stirred into the soul—one of peace and assurance. When leaders realize that God genuinely loves and cares for them (Ps 8:4; Nah 1:7; 1 Pet 5:7), they live with souls full of hope, assurance, security, and confidence and become "overflowing fountains"—giving rather than taking, refreshing rather than stifling.[88]

---

84. Hart, "Minister's Personal Growth." He reports that 23 percent of pastors surveyed had engaged in inappropriate sexual behavior.

85. Kruger, *Great Dance*, 71.

86. Ibid., 100.

87. Ibid., 101.

88. Ibid., 103.

Part 2: A Theology of the Trinitarian Leadership Dance

The first warm-up in preparation for transformational leadership is embracing one's identity as God's beloved child. A leader's identity must be rooted in the knowledge of the Father's adoption and not in the work of leadership or in service to God. When a leader's identity is based on work, that leader is driven by performance and insecurity rather than the security of being deeply loved and totally accepted by God.

Leaders, who will face constant criticism, must know the truth of the little caption: "I know I'm special, because God don't make no junk."[89] Relying on the Scripture that says, "I am fearfully and wonderfully made" (Ps 139:14), leaders will have courage to stand in the face of opposition. Acceptance, belonging, and security are realized when leaders discover the Father's unconditional love. The Father has entered into a covenant of faithfulness and commits himself to each believer's well-being, growth, and destiny. When leaders are embraced by the love of the Father, there is confidence that nothing can ever make God love them more—or less.

The Worth of the Son

In the original creation, Adam and Eve enjoyed a sense of safety and security. They were completely cared for, as all their needs were provided (Gen 1:29–30). Sadly, after the fall, their predominantly positive sense of being cared for and provided for was replaced with a negative sense of guilt and shame. No longer were their needs provided for, but Adam now had to endure "painful toil" as he worked the land (Gen 3:17). Eve also experienced "greatly increased pain" in childbearing (Gen 3:16). Their sense of self-worth, which came from being created in the image of God, was shattered. Similarly, many leaders today have a very fragile sense of self-worth and wrestle with esteem issues. Some question God's care for and value of them as people. These leaders must recognize their incredible value and worth as God's children, due to God's sacrifice of his Son.

The second prerequisite in warming up for the trinitarian leadership dance is understanding one's value in God's eyes. Only something incredibly valuable is ever considered lost. If a penny is dropped, it is not missed; however, if a diamond from an engagement ring falls out, a frantic search to recover it ensues immediately. The diamond is worth much more than a penny—not only monetarily but also sentimentally. By declaring, "For

---

89. I viewed a poster with this caption while visiting inmates at a penitentiary in Kingston, Ontario, on October 15, 1989.

The Trinitarian Dance as a Model

the Son of Man came to seek and to save what was lost" (Luke 19:10), Jesus states an incredible truth: humans matter a great deal to God.

To accept one's worth in God's eyes offers great value to leaders, whose self-worth will be challenged and battered in the fight to faithfully proclaim and witness to God's kingdom on earth and bring about positive lasting transformation in the organizations and systems that they lead. If leaders do not have their self-worth restored by accepting the price paid by the Son, they always will wrestle with esteem issues. It is precisely because so many leaders are blinded to their identity and worth that many search to fulfill these human needs through wrong means. Only by warming up everyday with these initial truths can leaders be prepared to join in the wonderful Trinitarian Dance of love and transformation in the world.

The Empowerment of the Holy Spirit

In the beginning, Adam and Eve were given the mandate to rule over the earth and to steward over God's creation (Gen 1:28). They were given dominion over all of God's creation, which gave them an incredible sense of significance. Additionally, they were able to carry out their responsibilities, because they walked in humble dependence with their Creator each day. In spite of all this, after sin entered the world, everything changed. "Dominion was replaced by weakness and helplessness."[90] Work became burdensome and wearisome. Their sense of significance, purpose, and meaning was lost. Fortunately, Christ reversed the effects of the fall, and believers now can overflow with a sense of strength and power by being filled with the Holy Spirit. The fruit of the Holy Spirit is boldness, strength, and self-control (Acts 4:31; Gal 5:23; 2 Tim 1:7).

Leaders who fail to experience the volcanic power of the Holy Spirit in life and ministry wrestle with power and control issues. Even the courageous Apostle Paul admitted his own feelings of inadequacy when he penned the following: "Not that we are competent in ourselves to claim anything for ourselves, but our competence comes from God. He has made us competent as ministers of a new covenant—not of the letter but of the Spirit; for the letter kills, but the Spirit gives life" (2 Cor 3:5–6).

Leaders must realize that their sustainability comes from their dependence on the Holy Spirit and not from working in their own strength and power. The power of the Holy Spirit is needed not only to overcome sin and

---

90. Anderson, *Victory Over the Darkness*, 38.

temptation but also to testify about the resurrected Christ, to reach out to the lost, and to minister in a dark world. Christian leaders empowered by the Holy Spirit can "do all things through Christ who strengthens them" (Phil 4:13). They have the very power that raised Jesus Christ from the dead working in them (Eph 1:19–20). In fact, the Greek word for "power," *dunamis*, used in Ephesians 1:19, is the same word from which the English word "dynamite" is derived.[91] The Holy Spirit must explode into the hearts of leaders to strengthen them to be able to do his will. It is the Holy Spirit who sustains leaders and guides them into their destiny, restoring their significance and meaning once again.

Psychologists claim that basic human needs—such as safety, security, belonging, and significance—must be met for humans to be creative, problem solving, or self-actualizing.[92] These needs are met when leaders take the time to warm up before entering into the leadership dance. Leaders must realize that they are lovable, valuable, and capable because the Trinity created, redeemed, and empowers them. These are the three essential truths that must be embraced in order to embark on the leadership journey with God. As Buxton writes:

> Lovingly, gently, and with infinite patience God teaches us the steps of the divine dance: when we stumble, he does not leave us helpless on the floor, nor does he point a disapproving finger at us. The Spirit who dwells within us, smiles over us as he reaches out a hand to pick us up and lead us on in the dance. . . . When we know that God is smiling at us with joy we are encouraged to learn the steps of his dance, and then creatively to choreograph new steps, new sequences, which flow out of his life within us. They are still his steps, but we are the ones who are bringing them into being.[93]

Confidence to participate in the leadership dance comes from being created in the Father's image, restored by the Son, and empowered by the Spirit. While these are only baby steps, they are indispensable to dancing the Trinitarian Dance of love.

---

91. BDAG, s.v. "*dunamis*."
92. Chapman, "Abraham Maslow's Hierarchy of Needs Motivational Model."
93. Buxton, *Dancing in the Dark*, 300–301.

THE TRINITARIAN DANCE AS A LEADERSHIP DANCE

The dream of the Trinity is to extend the fellowship of joy, beauty, laughter, creativity, knowledge, insights, music, intimacy, poetry, goodness, and glory enjoyed by the Father, Son, and Spirit.[94] Jesus came to make all of life a dance, including leadership. However, instead of skipping to a bountiful, overflowing, and joyful tune, leaders are tripping over countless concerns, stomping on toes, and weighed down by too many responsibilities, budgets, meetings, tasks, building plans, timelines, burdens, personnel, reports, concerns, emails, criticisms, projects, and cares.

By exploring the Trinity's leadership movements—demonstration, choreography, orchestration, and performance—leaders can learn the basic structure and steps of God's leadership dance. These movements are not rigid and fixed; rather, they are like recurring themes and motifs that weave in and out of the poem of leadership. Within each, there are three steps. Emerging leaders will gain familiarity with twelve leadership capacities contained within the four movements of the dance. Apprentices of the Trinity need to practice these twelve steps and dance them creatively to effortlessly join in the transformational mission of God in their own context.

Demonstration

Contrary to what the word suggests, the movement of demonstration not only happens prior to the other three movements but also occurs during them. The Father, Son, and Spirit demonstrate what joy, delight, mutual love, honor, and respect they share with one another. Their demonstration of holiness, balance, and trustworthiness reveals that the Trinity is God, that his plan is good, and that his purposes are sure. In the same way, leaders consistently must demonstrate that they are trustworthy, balanced, and whole. Demonstration gives them credibility and the moral authority to lead. These qualities will assist them greatly in a relativistic culture, where there is no guiding absolute truth. Their commitment to truth will increase their credibility. Integrity will shine like a beacon in a world that tolerates duplicity. In fact, leaders who fail to consistently demonstrate the qualities of wholeness, balance, and trust generate distrust, imbalance, and dysfunction—which gradually ripple throughout the organizations they lead.

---

94. Kruger, *Great Dance*, 26.

Part 2: A Theology of the Trinitarian Leadership Dance

Choreography

Choreography involves discerning with others God's vision, values, and strategies. The triune God has revealed a clear and compelling vision, offered biblical values as the guide, and acted in accordance with a mutually agreed upon plan. These three facets of choreography provide the triune God with clear direction towards his ultimate goal: the restoration of all things to their original design. Correspondingly, leadership teams who cast a clear vision, create mutually shared values, and develop a clear strategy are able to achieve their goals consistently. These skills will help Canadian leaders deal with the individualism and isolation that permeates Canadian culture. People will rally behind a clear vision and find hope in movement toward clearly defined goals. Shared values result in a greater sense of ownership and participation for all involved in their creation.

Orchestration

Participating in the transformational mission of God requires patience and persistence. The Trinity has exhibited this patience and persistence in his dealings with humanity. From the Trinity, one discerns healthy patterns of two-way communication, conflict resolution, and forgiveness—the three steps involved in orchestration. These practices can effect tremendous change and offer Canadian leaders greater humility, sensitivity, and facility in witnessing to God's kingdom. These leadership practices will assist in creating authentic community that speaks a message of hope to a fragmented and broken society.

Performance

The fourth movement of the leadership dance is performance, which involves teamwork, caring relationships, and empowerment. Understanding the dance of the Trinity equips leaders for genuine teamwork. The mutual honor, respect, joy, and delight that each member of the Trinity display towards one another reflects the quality of caring relationships that are essential for transformational change. Most importantly, the goal of the Trinity's leadership is to empower humanity to become like Christ. Likewise, leaders must create synergistic teams, exhibit caring relationships, and empower others to become all that they were created to be. These three aspects of

The Trinitarian Dance as a Model

the leadership dance contribute to building an authentic caring community that will address Canadians' passive disengagement with their world.

The Trinitarian Dance of love provides a powerful metaphor for the construction of a Christian leadership model. The central goal of the Christian life is to participate in God's love, or to "abide in Christ" (John 15:4; 1 John 4:16). Gregory Boyd asserts, "God's desire is for us to . . . dance with the Father, Son, and Holy Spirit in the joyful celebration of their eternal love and life."[95] Christian leaders, therefore, must learn how to dance this dance of love in order to invite others to participate in God's mission and to be effective in bringing about lasting transformation in the organizations and systems that they lead. Embracing the movements that emanate from the Trinitarian Dance will restore integrity, dignity, and celebration to a battered, marginalized, and neglected institution—the church.

Experiencing the love of the Father, the grace of the Lord Jesus Christ, and the power of the Holy Spirit is the warm-up essential to learning the Trinity's leadership dance and the blessing needed to sustain leaders throughout the challenges of leading change. Understanding the four movements of the leadership dance enables leaders to keep in step with how the Holy Spirit is leading and guiding in their unique situation. Practicing the three aspects of each movement gives leaders a greater capacity to engage in the dance of love and life with the Trinity and to participate in the ministry of Christ in the world today. In this way, the Master will move through leaders to effect life transformation and keep them in tune as instruments of his grace.

---

95. Boyd, *Repenting of Religion*, 15.

5

Movement I: Demonstration

Demonstration is more about authenticity than perfection, more about reality than idealism, and more about partnering than suspicion. It involves three aspects: growing in wholeness, increasing in balance, and building trust. No one is completely whole, but one can grow from year to year. There are few who are totally balanced, but one can nurture a healthy respect for boundaries. Even fewer are entirely trustworthy, yet one can grow and cultivate trust.

This chapter examines how the Father, Son, and Holy Spirit each uniquely model these three essential aspects of leadership. The Trinity consistently exhibits integrity, respect for limits, and dependability in his character and actions. Similarly, leaders must continually increase their capacity for wholeness, balance, and trustworthiness. Demonstration is indispensable to leadership.

UNDERSTANDING WHOLENESS

Wholeness is the opposite of a divided or wounded life. Wholeness does not mean perfection but genuinely embracing one's true self—weaknesses and strengths alike. God, by definition, is whole. The Trinity is complete, fulfilled, and satisfied. When Jews refer to God as one (Deut 6:4), they make a fundamental statement about the wholeness and completeness of God. God is one, but he is not lonely or needy in any way. God does not require believers' faith, love, or even participation in his plan to fulfill him. The

Movement I: Demonstration

Trinity is utterly and completely satisfied in the dance of love among Father, Son, and Holy Spirit. Each member of the Trinity distinctively displays wholeness by bringing *shalom*, resting in identity, and reflecting holiness.

God, the Father

In the Old Testament, God is referred to as *Yahweh Shalom*, or "The LORD Is Peace" (Judg 6:24; Ps 29:11; Isa 9:6; 26:3; 30:15; 32:17; Ezek 34:25; 37:26; Mic 5:5). The Hebrew word *shalom* means more than "an absence of strife"; it connotes the idea of completeness, wholeness, harmony, fulfillment, soundness, safety, security, prosperity, wellness, welfare, tranquility, perfection, fullness, rest, and even health.[1] *Shalom* is one of the most important theological words in the Old Testament, occurring over 250 times.[2] Implicit in *shalom* is the idea of unimpaired relationships with others and fulfillment in one's undertakings. This is the key to demonstrating wholeness and is expressed in the perichoretic nature of the Trinity.

Many Old Testament leaders experienced God's peace in their encounters with him. Gideon worshipped God as *Yahweh Shalom* after God declared to him, "Peace! Do not be afraid" (Judg 6:23–24). Gideon realized that one cannot be at peace and be afraid, anxious, or insecure at the same time. When God comes, *shalom* casts out fear.

The Father conveys *shalom* to his people. God has made a covenant of *shalom* (Ezek 34:25; 37:26), blesses his people with *shalom* (Ps 29:11), and speaks *shalom* over them (Num 6:24–26; Ps 85:8). The result of righteousness is *shalom* (Isa 32:17) and those who trust in God will be kept in *shalom shalom*, "perfect peace" (Isa 9:6).

The Father also brings *shalom* to creation. All of creation shouts his glory and displays his splendor (Ps 19:1–4). The Creator rests content in all that he has made and declares it very good (Gen 1:31). At the moment, God's perfect world has been frustrated, "groaning as in the pains of childbirth" due to the fall (Gen 3; Rom 8:20–22). It eagerly awaits the restoration of God's perfect *shalom* with Christ's second coming (Rom 8:20–22; 2 Pet 3:13; Rev 21:1).

Father God, then, demonstrates wholeness by bringing peace, contentment, fulfillment, prosperity, and enjoyment to his people and his creation. Surely a deeper intimacy with the Father will bring greater wholeness and

---

1. BDB, s.v. "shalom;" see also TWOT, s.v. "shalom."
2. TWOT, s.v. "shalom." BDB lists 237 uses.

peace to leaders who seek to bring *shalom* into their spheres of influence. This is one of the first objectives of Christian leadership development: to bring developing leaders into deeper intimacy with the Father, Son, and Holy Spirit and free them from everything that blocks God's peace and wholeness in their lives. Leaders must rest securely in the love of the Father to increasingly experience God's *shalom* in their everyday lives.

Jesus Christ, the Son

Just as the Father is perfectly whole, the Son also is completely whole. Wholeness does not imply that Jesus was static, since he grew "in wisdom, stature, and in favor with God and humanity" (Luke 2:52). Instead, Jesus found his identity neither in his power as God nor in his mission of salvation for the world; rather, he found it in his relationship with the Father. At age twelve, he knew his identity and explained to his earthly parents the necessity for his presence in his Father's house (Luke 2:49). Jesus did not "put on" Sonship at his baptism; rather, he embraced his identity as Son throughout his life, death, and resurrection and modeled how one can find fulfillment and satisfaction by becoming God's child (John 1:12). Leighton Ford reflects on the implications of Christ's Sonship: "I am impressed that before Jesus had done a single thing to start his ministry, God said he was pleased with who he was. It says to us that God is far more interested in our being than our doing, in what we are than in our actions."[3]

Jesus rests completely in his identity as the Son. His Sonship is a common theme throughout the Gospels. In the Gospel of John alone, Jesus refers to the Father nearly a hundred times.[4] He rests securely in the Father's love (John 3:35; 5:20), delights in the life of the Father (John 5:26), and refuses to deny this relationship despite how the religious authorities raged over his claims (John 5:18, 23). He stands in the Father's presence (John 1:14, 18; 6:46; 8:38), speaks only what he hears from the Father (John 8:38; 12:49), and does only what the Father does (John 5:19, 21). He completely trusts the Father (Luke 23:46; 24:49) and is zealous for his Father's reputation (John 2:16). All that Jesus embodies in the incarnation flows from his intimate relationship with the Father. His life of Sonship exemplifies all that it means for humans to be complete and whole in their identity as children of God (1 John 3:1).

3. Ford, *Transforming Leadership*, 41.
4. *Bible Gateway*, s.v. "Father."

Movement I: Demonstration

Moreover, all that Jesus accomplished on the cross is the "supreme expression of faithfulness to his own identity."[5] On the cross, the completely human Christ embodied the brokenness, estrangement, and alienation of fallen humanity while at the same time maintaining his relationship with the Father and his identity as the Son. Kruger describes this paradox: "He bore the violent contradiction in his own being, and he resolved it . . . by dying to his Adamic flesh, by crucifying it on Calvary. For in no other way could he live out his fellowship with his Father—as the incarnate Son—except through putting to death the flesh of Adam."[6] By embracing the sin of humanity, Jesus embraced humanity's suffering, pain, and isolation—all that is the antithesis of wholeness and life. By being faithful to the will of his Father, Jesus crucified everything that robs humanity of the wholeness, peace, and joy that God has destined for his children.

In his resurrection, Jesus continued to find wholeness in his identity as the Son of God and in his dependence on the Father. The resurrected Jesus revealed his wholeness to the disciples, appearing to them over a period of forty days (Acts 1:3). He showed them that living in wholeness is not a life devoid of scars (John 20:27), but one that completely eliminates "Adamic flesh" and embraces the wholeness, joy, and abundant life of the Father. Similarly, Christian leaders must follow this example of their Commander-in-Chief by resting securely in their identity as God's beloved children and depending on their relationship with the Father to discern their unique calling and assignment in this world.

The Holy Spirit

All the Spirit does brings health, peace, and contentment, as indicated by the fruit of the Holy Spirit (Gal 5:22). The Holy Spirit gives life (John 6:63), teaches all things (John 14:26), and reminds believers of all that Jesus taught, including Christ's gift of peace (John 14:27). The Holy Spirit is also the Spirit of adoption (Gal 4:6; Rom 8:15). He confirms one's identity as God's beloved child and repudiates feelings of abandonment (John 14:18). The Holy Spirit brings wholeness and peace by revealing God's holiness, giving life, and assisting believers in embracing their true identity as God's children.

---

5. Kruger, *Great Dance*, 42.
6. Ibid.

Part 2: A Theology of the Trinitarian Leadership Dance

Wholeness is related to holiness, the defining characteristic of the Spirit. I will never forget the freedom and release that came to me, a legalist and a perfectionist at the time, when I initially grasped the meaning of the Scripture: "Be holy, as I am holy" (Lev 19:2; 1 Pet 1:15–16). My Hebrew professor explained, "This verse means: Just as I, the Lord your God, am completely and utterly God—You, human being, in all that you are, be completely and utterly human. Just as I embrace all that my divinity entails, so you, human, embrace all that your true humanity entails."[7] In other words, holiness does not mean unachievable perfection. Certainly holiness involves purity, but not white-gloved morality—an unattainable standard that leaves one feeling guilty for not measuring up. A new degree of freedom ushered into my soul that day. No longer did holiness mean flawlessness (as if I could have attained perfection), but rather it meant becoming whole. In that class, I received a small glimpse of the beauty, glory, and holiness of the dance of the Trinity.

MAINTAINING BALANCE

The next step in the Trinity's dance of leadership is seeking balance among planning, action, and rest. Balance entails living a radically honest life: honesty about one's strengths, weaknesses, and desires. Just as balance is necessary for dancers not to step on their partner's toes, balance is needed in Christian leadership to demonstrate the Trinity's power in ordinary lives. The God of truth models balance by resting after creation, respecting natural human limitations, and empowering believers to live balanced lives in harmony with God's rhythms of grace.

God, the Father

Ĕlōhîm describes God in the work of creation and refers to the true and sovereign God.[8] The prefix *'ēl* means "mighty one," "strength," or "mighty God" and refers to God's greatness or superiority over all other gods.[9] He is called *ha'ēl haggādôl*, the great God (Jer 32:18; Ps 77:13; 95:3); *ha'el 'osehpele*, God doing wonders (Ps 77:14); and *'ēl ḥay*, the living God (Josh 3:10; 1

---

7. Remin, "Hebrew Exegesis."
8. TWOT, s.v. "ēl," "ĕlōh," "ĕlōhîm."
9. Ibid.

Movement I: Demonstration

Sam 17:26, 36; 2 Kgs 19:4, 16; Ps 42:2; 84:2; Isa 37:4; Jer 10:10, 23:36; Dan 6:20, 26; Hos 1:10).[10] Despite being the all-powerful, almighty Creator and Sustainer of the universe, God chooses to rest. The One, who has more than enough reserves to govern the entire universe, still conserves his energies on the seventh day (Gen 2:2). More than providing a model for humanity, the mighty God respects the rhythm of life. "There is a time for everything," the teacher of Ecclesiastes instructs (Eccl 3:1–8). God the Father, who set these times and from the beginning, chose to introduce a rhythm of resting one day and working six days.

In fact, on the first full day of existence for Adam and Eve, God rested. God created man and woman on the sixth day, blessed them, and gave them the imperative to rule over the earth (Gen 1:28). One might imagine that they were eager to get to work and to obey God's command. Yet, on the first full day on earth, God required that they rest. From this there is an important principle: humans are to work from rest and not rest from work.[11] God wanted humanity to enjoy the perichoretic love that he enjoyed from the beginning, before they got to work. His desire for humanity is for people to enter into his perichoretic rest and experience work as stemming from rest. Leupp describes this respite as "the rest that each Person feels in the company of the other two [and is like] the welcoming and comfortable dwelling together of the three divine persons."[12]

Undoubtedly, rest is of utmost importance to the Father who commanded the Israelites to rest on the Sabbath (Exod 20:8; 31:4–5; Deut 5:12), who gave his people rest (Josh 21:44; 1 Kgs 5:4), and who promised rest to those who seek shelter under the shadow of his wing (Ps 91:1). He instructed the Israelites to give the land a rest (Lev 25:2–5), commanded his prophets to remind his people about their Sabbath rests (Isa 56:2, 6; 58:13; Jer 17:21), and was angered by them for not entering into his rest (Ps 95:11; Heb 3:11). God longs to see people experience his rest (Ps 62:1, 5; Isa 30:15; Jer 6:16). By his incarnation, Jesus demonstrated how to receive God's rest and invites all to come to him to dwell in that rest (Matt 11:28). Moreover, the Spirit urges Christians to "make every effort to enter into that rest" (Heb 4:10–11). Indeed, rest is fundamental to the Father who designed humanity to abide in his love and live in his rest. Leaders who fail to abide by God's

---

10. Ibid.
11. Breen and Kallestad, *Passionate Church*, 67.
12. Leupp, *Knowing the Name of God*, 162.

Part 2: A Theology of the Trinitarian Leadership Dance

rhythms of grace and rest miss the abundant life that the Father has created for them to enjoy.

Jesus Christ, the Son

Jesus understood and respected his human needs and human limitations while on earth. He was able to create and sustain what Richard A. Swenson describes as margin. Margin is simply this:

> Power—[minus] Load, where power refers to factors such as skills, time, emotional strength, physical strength, spiritual vitality, finances, social supports, and education and load refers to internal factors (such as personal expectations and emotional disabilities) and external factors (such as work, relational problems and responsibilities, financial obligations, and civic involvement).[13]

One may be tempted to think that Jesus had an unfair advantage, since his power was infinitely greater than ours; however, it is important to consider his load.

Emotional

When Jesus became incarnate, he took on and experienced the full range of human emotion—from euphoric joy to despair. He was "full of joy" over hearing the success of the seventy disciples whom he had trained and sent out to announce the kingdom (Luke 10:21); he "wept" at his good friend's death (John 11:35); he was "overwhelmed with sorrow and troubled to the point of death" in Gethsemane (Matt 26:38); he was frustrated with the "unbelieving generation" (Luke 9:41); and he was angry at the temple traders who distracted and even may have obstructed people from genuine worship (John 2:14–16). In every situation, Jesus responded appropriately and authentically to his emotions.[14]

To replenish his emotional reserves, he unashamedly chose twelve disciples for the focus of his life work. Of the twelve, he gravitated closer to three (Peter, James, and John), choosing only these men to accompany him on special occasions.[15] Of these three, there was one whom he favored

---

13. Swenson, *Margin*, 92.
14. Wilson, *Released from Shame*, 197.
15. The healing of Jairus' daughter (Luke 8:51), the transfiguration (Luke 9:28–36),

over the rest. He is referred to in John's Gospel as "the disciple whom Jesus loved" (John 21:20). Jesus also cultivated friendships outside his band of disciples, eating at many different people's homes and spending time with them.[16]

Physical

Jesus respected the physical limitations that the Father placed on him in the incarnation. While he was a child, he chose to go home and be obedient to his parents (Luke 2:52). He slept when his body needed rest (Matt 8:24). He left a pressing crowd to get some much needed food and rest, and he instructed his disciples to do the same (Mark 6:31). He respected his body's need for physical food, even though he had a more vital dependence on the Father than on physical food for strength (John 4:32–34). Being fully human, he depended on the Father as his source to look after all of the legitimate human needs that he experienced while on earth: intimacy, proper nutrition, rest, spiritual vitality, and physical exercise.

Time

Jesus was not a workaholic, which is the "acceptable sin" of evangelicalism. He was not "overdependent," "hyperactive," or "Baptisticly busy."[17] He respected his need for solitude and quiet time with his Father God (Mark 1:35) and the need to live from that central relationship with the Father. On the Sabbath, after ministering in the synagogue, Jesus went to the home of Peter's mother-in-law for the Sabbath meal. He healed her and then enjoyed an afternoon of fellowship, not ministering again until "the sun was setting" (Luke 4:38–40). He did not minister morning, noon, and night. He lived a balanced lifestyle.

As well, he remained cognizant of proper moments. He understood that "there is a time for everything and a season for every activity under heaven" (Eccl 3:1). He appreciated the difference between *chronos* time (chronological time) and *kairos* time (opportune time) and chose to live by the latter. When his brothers pushed him to go to Judea to the Feast of

---

and Gethsemane (Mark 14:33).

16. Lazarus and his two sisters (Luke 10:38–39; John 11:5; 12:1–2).
17. Wilson, *Released from Shame*, 121–57.

Tabernacles, he replied, "The right time for me has not yet come" (John 7:1–8). The Gospel of John twice declares that people could not seize him, because his hour had not yet come (John 7:30; 8:20). When his mother invited him to change the water into wine, he insisted, "My hour has not yet come" (John 2: 4). Yet, on the night of his arrest, he knew that "the hour had come" (John 13:1; 16:32). He was never in a hurry, never busy, and never overburdened. He invited all who follow him to take up his easy yoke and his burden, which is light (Matt 11:28–30).

The Holy Spirit

The Holy Spirit enables balance by empowering ordinary believers to live within divinely ordained rhythms of grace. Those overflowing with the Holy Spirit are filled with great joy, unconditional love, and abiding peace (Gal 5:22). By faith in Christ, they have become children of God (John 1:12), having been birthed from above by the Holy Spirit (John 3:5–8). They now have the basic nature of the Father, since the Father has passed on to them his nature, "as any parent does."[18] Their old nature still exists, but they have trained themselves to disregard it. Putting off the old nature is as easy as taking off soiled clothes at the end of the day, and putting on the new nature is as natural as putting on fresh garments in the morning (Eph 4:22–24). The Holy Spirit does not make them perfect; in fact, such followers of Christ have learned that masks of perfection are not needed anymore. They know that God is their protector, so they have given up all efforts of self-protection and entrust themselves into the loving Father's care. However, they are completely different; their distinctiveness is found primarily on the "inside" of their life. Every aspect of their lives is transformed by the Holy Spirit's touch.[19]

The Holy Spirit reveals the Father and the Son to believers. In fact, an understanding of the Trinity encourages balance in one's relationship with each member of the Godhead. "The Christian life is like a three-legged stool," writes Johnson, "knock out one leg and the stool wobbles and falls."[20] Each person of the Godhead connects with individuals in real and personal ways. Therefore, Christians can develop greater balance in their relationship with the Father, Son, and Holy Spirit by focusing on the person of the

---

18. Willard, *Renovation of the Heart*, 218.

19. Ibid., 218–20. Here Willard sketches a picture of these transformed believers.

20. Johnson, *Experiencing the Trinity*, 53.

Trinity with whom they are least familiar and learning from Christians in other traditions.[21]

ESTABLISHING TRUST

In Hebrew, there are three names which reflect God's trustworthy nature: *'ēl 'ōlam*, the eternal God (Gen 21:33); *'ēl 'eme*, the God of Truth (Ps 31:5; Deut 32:4; Isa 65:16); and *ha' el hanne'eman*, the Faithful God (Deut 7:9).[22] The Trinity is timeless, and his principles are universal. From everlasting to everlasting, he is God; his eternal nature is consistent with his actions in the world. Those who walk in his ancient paths find rest for their souls (Jer 6:16). He is the God of truth; all truth comes from him and is found in him. He is faithful and true, utterly reliable and dependable. Consequently, the Trinity displays trustworthiness in three ways: genuineness, veracity, and faithfulness.

Genuineness: Being True

In a world that cries out for authenticity, integrity, and consistency, one truth stands out: the Trinity is the eternally true God. God is unchanging (Ps 102:26–27; 33:11; Mal 3:6; Jas 1:17), meaning that there is no quantitative or qualitative change in God; he is constant. God cannot increase quantitatively in anything, since he is complete. God's nature cannot undergo any modification, since he is perfect. God's intentions and purposes do not change; he is consistent. God is stable and sure: the same yesterday, today, and forever (Heb 13:8). He will act as he has promised; he will fulfill his commitments. This understanding, however, need not suggest that God is static. Erikson clarifies: "Some interpretations of the doctrine of divine constancy . . . have drawn upon the Greek idea of immobility and sterility. This makes God inactive. The biblical view is not that God is static but stable. He is active and dynamic, but in a way which is stable and consistent with his nature. God is dependable."[23]

Moreover, there is an intrinsic link between how God acts in salvation history (the "economic" Trinity) and the internal nature of God (the

---

21. Schwarz, *Color Your World with Natural Church Development*, 46–79.
22. TWOT, s.v. "ēl," "ĕlōah," "ĕlōhîm."
23. Erickson, *Christian Theology*, 278.

"immanent" Trinity). This unity often is referred to as "Rahner's rule."[24] The way God appears to humanity is the way God exists in his own inner life. God is in himself the same God who orchestrates salvific history. This internal/external integrity reflects an undivided and true God.

People trusted Jesus because he had integrity. He taught "as one who had authority" (Mark 1:22), cast out demons (Mark 1:27), and healed the sick (Mark 1:34). He lived a holy and sinless life (John 8:46; 1 Pet 2:22; 1 John 3:5; 2 Col 5:21; Matt 27:54). He demonstrated power over natural forces. He stilled a raging storm (Mark 4:41), turned water into wine (John 2:1–11), fed five thousand with five loaves and two fish (Matt 14:13–21), and even raised the dead (John 11:38–44). He demonstrated the Creator's power over sickness and disease and made the lame to walk, the dumb to speak, and the blind to see. Even his own resurrection from the grave demonstrated God's power over death. Everything Jesus did demonstrated his consistency with everything he claimed. His character displayed a life that was undivided and whole.

The Holy Spirit is as trustworthy as the Father and the Son, because he is "another of the same kind" (John 14:16). He is referred to as the Spirit of the Father (Matt 10:20), the Spirit of Jesus (Acts 16:7), the Spirit of the Son (Gal 4:6), the Spirit of Jesus Christ (Phil 1:19), and the Spirit of Christ (1 Pet 1:11). He is the Spirit of glory and of God (1 Pet 4:14). He is the Father's good gift (Luke 11:13), who testifies about Jesus (John 15:24) and speaks only what he hears (John 16:13). He has promised to take from what belongs to Jesus and make it known to his disciples (John 16:15). The Holy Spirit exhibits integrity and genuineness in his power to save and perform miracles in a person's life. Christians joyfully can affirm the Holy Spirit's divine nature from the truths revealed in the Scriptures and trust in his genuine and true nature as God.

Veracity: Telling the Truth

God the Father speaks the truth. Unlike humans, when God speaks he does not lie or change his mind (Num 28:19; 1 Sam 15:29; Heb 7:21). He declares, "I, the Lord, speak the truth; I declare what is right" (Isa 45:19). He speaks truth, because his understanding knows no limit. No one can ever take God's place; no one is superior in logic or reasoning. The Father's wisdom is comprehensive, not lacking in judgment or understanding in

24. Rahner, *Trinity*, 33.

any way (Isa 55:8–9). Even the keen intellect of the scholarly Apostle Paul recognized God's thinking as brilliant and wrote:

> Oh, the depth of the riches of the wisdom and knowledge of God! How unsearchable his judgments, and his paths beyond tracing out! "Who has known the mind of the Lord? Or who has been his counselor?" "Who has ever given to God, that God should repay him?" For from him and through him and to him are all things. To him be the glory forever! Amen. (Rom 11:33–36)

Jesus told the truth that he heard from God (John 8:40). One of his favorite sayings was "I tell you the truth," which is used over seventy-five times in the Gospels.[25] He taught that the Father must be worshipped in Spirit and in truth (John 4:23–24). He was a "man of truth," for he worked for the honor of the Father and did not labor towards his own public honor (John 7:18). He proclaimed that if one followed his teachings, one would know the truth and be set free (John 8:31–32). Jesus bore witness to the truth from God, and everyone on the side of truth listens to him (John 3:32–33; 18:37). John the Baptist testified to the truth about Jesus (John 5:33), as did many other eyewitnesses (John 9:25; 19:35; 21:24).

Jesus not only spoke the truth, he lived it (John 1:14, 17). He said, "Anyone who lives by the truth comes into the light, so that it may be seen plainly that what he has done has been done through God" (John 3:21). He lived in the light—claiming that he was "the way, the truth and the life" (John 14: 6)—and invited followers to put their trust in him (John 12:36; 14:1). He prayed for his disciples that the Father would sanctify them in the truth (John 17:17). He sent the Spirit of truth (John 14:17; 15:26; 16:13) to guide believers into all truth (John 16:13).

The Holy Spirit is the "Spirit of Truth" (John 14:17; 15:26; 16:13; 1 John 4:6; 5:6), sent to guide believers into all truth (John 16:13), and speaks the truth (Acts 28:25). The Spirit teaches all things and reminds disciples of everything that Jesus said (John 14:26). He is also the Spirit of holiness (Rom 1: 4), who gives wisdom and revelation (Acts 6:3, 10; Eph 1:17), because he is a witness to the truth (Acts 5:32). The Holy Spirit is essential, because no one can enter the kingdom without being born of the Spirit (John 3: 5–6), who is the deposit guaranteeing what is to come (2 Cor 1:22; 5:5; Eph 1:14). The Spirit sanctifies (Rom 15:16), renews (Titus 3:5), and brings believers to surrender to Christ's leadership (1 Cor 12:3). Leadership without the Spirit of God is death, but following the lead of the Spirit brings

---

25. *Bible Gateway*, s.v. "I tell you the truth."

life and peace (Rom 8: 5–8). God gives the Spirit freely without limit to those who ask (John 3:34), so there is no reason not to fully receive God's gift of the Holy Spirit.

Faithfulness: Proving True

The Father demonstrates trustworthiness by proving himself to be faithful. God is described as "a faithful God, who does no wrong" (Deut 32:4), "slow to anger, abounding in love and faithfulness" (Exod 34:6; Ps 86:15), and "a faithful God, keeping his covenant of love" (Deut 7:9). To the faithful, he shows himself faithful (2 Sam 22:25; Ps 18:25), all his ways are loving and faithful (Ps 25:10), and his faithfulness reaches to the skies (Ps 36:5; 57:10; 108:4). Like a garment, God's faithfulness surrounds him (Ps 89:8), goes before him (Ps 89:14), and is a shield and rampart to all who trust in him (Ps 91:4). The works of his hands and all that he does are faithful and just (Ps 111:7–8), he is faithful to all his promises (Ps 145:13), and his faithfulness continues throughout all generations (Ps 100:5; 117:2; 119:90). No one can ever doubt God's faithfulness, for it has been established in heaven itself (Ps 89:2). The Father is an utterly trustworthy God and deserves all praise, glory, and trust (Ps 146:6, 10).

Just as the Father is faithful, so too the Son is faithful, making him completely reliable. He is loyal to the One who appointed him (Heb 3:2), trustworthy as a son over God's house (Heb 3:5), and keeps his promises (Heb 10:23). He remains true to his word to forgive sins (1 John 1:9) and serves as a reliable witness to God's truth (Rev 1:5). He is the God of the Amen, or the God of truth (Rev 3:14; Isa 65:16), and the rider on the white horse whose name is Faithful and True (Rev 19:11). Moreover, he has been loyal to the Father, submitting himself even unto death (Phil 2: 8). His resurrection from the dead proves his faithfulness—three times he predicted that he would die and rise again (Mark 8:31; 9:31; 10:33–34), and he did.

Likewise, the Holy Spirit proves himself true in his faithfulness in the ongoing work of sanctification and empowerment for ministry in the lives of believers. He is ever devoted to empowering believers to minister in Christ's name and to become like Christ. The Holy Spirit anointed Jesus to "preach good news to the poor, to proclaim freedom for the prisoners and recovery of sight for the blind, to release the oppressed, and to proclaim the year of the Lord's favor" (Luke 4:18–19). Similarly, Spirit-filled believers will do "even greater things," for they rely on the same Spirit as Christ (John

Movement I: Demonstration

14:12). They need not worry about what they will say, because the Holy Spirit will teach them what to say (Luke 12:12). The Spirit enables believers to see visions and dreams (Acts 2:17; 2 Pet 1:21), because he is the "Spirit of prophecy" (Rev 19:10). The Spirit's anointing makes believers speak the Word of God boldly (Acts 4: 31), gives spiritual gifts to all believers (1 Cor 12:1–31), and fills them with the same power that raised Jesus Christ from the dead (Gal 4:29; Eph 3:16). This anointing is what enables leaders to lead with God's wisdom and strength.

More significant than the extraordinary, the Holy Spirit faithfully transforms believers in their ordinary lives to become more like Christ. He enables believers to know that God is in them (1 John 3:24), grants unity (Eph 4:3), and testifies to the truth (Heb 10:15). The Holy Spirit convicts of sin (John 16:8; 1 Thess 1:5), resulting in greater boldness, power, love, and self-control (2 Tim 1:7). His work leads to obedience in Jesus Christ (1 Pet 1:2), bringing complete freedom (2 Cor 3:17). The Holy Spirit pours God's love into believers' hearts (Rom 5:5) and infuses them with joy (Luke 10:21), life (John 6:63; Rom 8: 6), power (Acts 1:8), peace (Rom 8:6), and hope (Rom 15:13). The Spirit reveals all things (1 Cor 2:10) so that believers can understand what God has freely given (1 Cor 2:12), especially that they are God's children (Rom 8:14–16; Gal 4:6). The Spirit of life sets believers free from the law of sin and death (Rom 8:2), helping them in their weaknesses and interceding for them (Rom 8:26; Phil 1:19). Believers are to be filled with the Spirit (Eph 5: 21), be led by the Spirit (Gal 5:18), and keep in step with the Spirit (Gal 5:21) so that there is less of them and more of Christ everyday (John 3:30). Being filled with the Holy Spirit gives leaders the perseverance to prove faithful and true.

The Trinity is completely genuine, faithful, and true. This makes him totally reliable, dependable, and trustworthy. He has demonstrated essential character traits that leaders must exhibit. The Father, Son, and Holy Spirit also have entrusted us with participating in his mission on earth. Therefore, we must become familiar with the other three movements of the trinitarian leadership dance in order to partner with the Trinity in accomplishing his purposes.

6

Movement II: Choreography

The second movement of the Trinitarian Dance is choreography, which involves vision, values, and strategy. Often leaders mistakenly think that choreography is the first priority of leadership, but demonstration is primary. Without the solid foundation of a character that is trustworthy, balanced, and whole, Christian leaders become no more than the play actors or hypocrites that Jesus strongly condemned (Matt 6:5, 16). However, character alone does not make a leader. One needs a compelling vision, a commitment to biblical values, and a realistic action plan. As God choreographs salvific history, each member of the Trinity is active in all three aspects of this movement: vision, values, and strategy.

DISCERNING THE TRIUNE GOD'S VISION

Vision is a clear mental picture of a preferred future. It is a reflection of God's mission to establish Christ's kingdom in every realm of society. It is "not dreaming the impossible dream, but dreaming the most possible dream."[1] A vision must be inspiring and change oriented.[2] The Trinity has envisioned a completely different reality for people than the one most currently experienced: life in the kingdom of God.

---

1. Additionally, a vision must be challenging, empowering, long-term, customized, detailed, people-oriented, and reveal a promising future, according to Barna, *Power of Vision*, 30.

2. Ibid., 96–104.

Movement II: Choreography

Sweet argues that vision has to do more with the ears than with the eyes: "Leadership is not first a 'vision' thing. Leadership is first a 'vibration' thing."[3] He encourages leaders to develop "not a seeing mind, but a hearing heart," because "leaders don't see a vision, they hear one."[4] If leaders are going to dance with the Trinity in participating with his plans and purposes, then they need to start listening to the music of the dance and to the singing of God's voice as he hums his intentions for seeking hearts to hear. When they do, vision will resonate deep in their hearts and souls. Carson Pue offers this reflection to his readers: "An effective vision resonates in people much the same way [as harmonics on a guitar]."[5]

Discerning God's vision is paramount in a developing leader's life, because without God's picture of a preferred future that leader will get sidetracked with less critical causes or follow a path set by others. Vision is not something that successful people create; rather it is received from God. Pue reminds leaders that "followers of Jesus who are called to lead are not self-made people on some personally concocted journey. Vision is God's taking you from one place to another for his purposes—not our own."[6] For some, receiving a vision comes instantaneously, directly from God as a result of prayer and sometimes fasting. For others, seeing the vision takes time. Bill Hybels affirms, "Sometimes it comes into focus piece by piece over a long period of time, like a confusing puzzle that finally makes sense."[7] Once leaders see clearly the vision God has for them, they are able to sacrifice their lives in pursuit of that call. Each member of the Trinity reveals God's vision for humanity in a unique and compelling way.

God's Vision: A Bride

Gene Edwards describes a love story between the Almighty and his beloved bride in *The Divine Romance*. He imagines how the eternal lover envisions a bride for himself before the foundation of the world: "It burst upon Him suddenly, this revelation. . . . That there could be two! An all-knowing God had brought forth a thought so exciting that even He trembled in its afterglow. Then, exulting in revelation, He consecrated His whole being to

---

3. Sweet, *Summoned to Lead*, 56.
4. Ibid., 57, 60.
5. Pue, *Mentoring* Leaders, 133.
6. Ibid., 80.
7. Hybels, *Courageous Leadership*, 33.

this one task: to have . . . a bride."⁸ God's vision for his bride provides motivation, direction, and anticipation for the acts of creation, redemption, sanctification, and Christ's second coming. All that God is doing, has done, and will do is to bring into reality this ultimate vision of a pure, spotless, radiant bride. Edwards envisions that day:

> The angels exult in holy delight. They recognize that form, for they have seen it once before in a brief moment of glory . . . long ago.
> Standing before them, is the Bride of the Lamb.
> She emerges into clear view, the radiance of her light and glory eclipsing all, save the throne of God. She stands before them robed in purity and holiness.
> For a moment all things else seem to vanish away in the presence of this holy and glorious bride. Suddenly, though, there appears in the distance a yet greater glory.
> None else but the King!
> As might two gleeful children, they run toward one another, and embrace in an exchange of divine love. With all else having already dissolved, the light of the glory of the two now melts into one.⁹

The Scriptures portray the Almighty as an eternal lover longing for his beloved. God's people are referred to as "the apple of his eye" (Deut 32:10) and as God's "treasured possession" (Mal 3:17), metaphors used between lovers. His very name is Jealous (Exod 20:4–6; 34:14; Deut 4:24; 5:9; 6:15; Josh 24:19) and reveals his fierce demand for the love of his people. God as an eternal lover who is searching for, longing for, jealous for, and fighting for his beloved, emerges as a dominant theme throughout the pages of Scripture.

The prophet Hosea and his wife, Gomer, vividly portray how God faithfully loves his people despite their adultery and rebellion. Just as Hosea woos his adulterous bride back to himself and loves her again, so the God of Israel woos his people back to himself and continues to faithfully love them (Hos 3:1). God's heart is broken by his people's unfaithfulness; however, he still leads them with "chords of human kindness," "lifts the yoke from their neck," and "bends down to feed them" (Hos 11:4). God's lovesick concern for his people is revealed poignantly in this declaration: "How can I give

---

8. Edwards, *Divine Romance*, 3–4.
9. Ibid., 202–3.

you up, Ephraim? How can I hand you over, Israel? . . . My heart is changed within me; all my compassion is aroused" (Hos 11:8).

Both the Old and New Testaments paint a picture of God's love using the metaphor of a bridegroom and a bride. God delights in his people like a bridegroom rejoices over his bride (Isa 6:5). God himself, through the prophet Jeremiah, declares the covenantal nature of his love: "I have loved you with an everlasting love; I have drawn you with unfailing kindness" (Jer 31:3). God demonstrates and proves this love by sending his only Son to die for the sins of humankind (John 3:16; Rom 5:8). Twice Jesus envisions the kingdom of heaven as a wedding feast (Matt 22:1–14; 25:1–13) and refers to himself as the bridegroom (Matt 9:15; Mark 2:19; Luke 5:34–35). John echoes Jesus' words, referring to himself only as a friend of the bridegroom but not the bridegroom (John 3:29). The Apostle Paul likens the tender relationship between husband and wife to the relationship between Christ and the church (Eph 5:25–27).

The image of a bride appears again in Revelation, where the second coming of Christ is celebrated as a bridegroom coming for his bride. Multitudes celebrate that the wedding of the Lamb has come and that the bride has made herself ready (Rev 19:7). John is given a vision of a new heaven and a new earth, in which the New Jerusalem is seen as "coming down out of heaven from God, prepared as a bride beautifully dressed for her husband" (Rev 21:2). Again the bride echoes the voice of the Spirit in inviting all to partake in the wedding feast by proclaiming, "Come" (Rev 22:17).

The church, comprised of all true believers throughout history, throughout all denominations, and throughout the world, is that beautiful bride. God has destined for her to be with him throughout all eternity due to his great love. Henri J. M. Nouwen believes that God's words "You are my Beloved," spoken to Jesus by the Father (found in Matt 3:16–17; Mark 1:10–11; Luke 3:21–22), reveal "the most intimate truth about all human beings, whether they belong to any particular tradition or not."[10] The Canadian church must see itself as God's beloved bride in order to experience this "most intimate truth" and know God's fierce love. When it does, it will overcome the feelings of isolation that are so prevalent in many urban cities and rural locations across the nation. The Canadian church has the unique privilege and opportunity to prepare the bride for the bridegroom's coming. When the Canadian church catches a glimpse of this vision and participates

---

10. Nouwen, *Life of the Beloved*, 30.

in the divine plan of winning souls to Christ and discipling them into maturity, it becomes more completely what God designed it to be.

Jesus' Vision: The Kingdom of God

Jesus came to earth to redeem God's precious bride (Gal 3:13). To cast the Father's vision, Christ needed to communicate a picture that humanity readily could embrace, so he focused on the rule and reign of God, the kingdom of heaven. God envisions a dance partner—a pure and spotless bride who is one with him. Fallen humanity, however, sees a kingdom—same vision, yet a different perspective. Looking upward to heaven, the bride sees her King; looking downward from heaven, the King envisions a bride. When the betrothed embraces her lover, the King receives his beloved partner in the eternal dance of love and life. Jesus, being fully human and fully divine, modeled what it means to dance with God in the darkness of this world and holds out his hand inviting all to join him in the dance. He is not only the "premier danseur" but also the Lord of the dance.

At the heart of Jesus' message was his teaching on the kingdom of God or the kingdom of heaven. Virtually every New Testament scholar agrees with this fact since the Gospels contain over one hundred verses about the kingdom.[11] The kingdom of God refers to God's own reign, or rule, and is "the range of his effective will, where what he wants done is done."[12] It was this vision of the kingdom that Jesus continually placed before his disciples in order to generate the creative tension needed to inspire them to desire more.

Throughout the pages of Scripture, the kingdom of God is a central theme. The Old and New Testaments declare that God's kingdom is everlasting and never will be overthrown (Dan 7:14; Ps 145:13; Heb 12:28). The psalmist proclaims the reality of God's kingdom ruling over all (Ps 103:19) and speaks of the majesty and glory of his reign (Pss 93, 97). While under siege from the Assyrians, King Hezekiah comforts himself with the knowledge that the Lord is the king over all the kingdoms of the earth (Isa 37:16). By seeking this God in prayer and crying out to him for deliverance, King Hezekiah obtained victory over King Sennacherib (Isa 37: 21–38). John the

---

11. Green et al., eds., *Dictionary of Jesus and the Gospels*, s.vv. "The kingdom of heaven." According to this source, "the Synoptic Gospels contain 76 different Kingdom sayings, or 103, including the parallels."

12. Willard, *Divine Conspiracy*, 25.

Movement II: Choreography

Baptist announced the coming kingdom as he prepared the way for the Messiah (Matt 3:2).

Jesus preached about the kingdom of God and instructed his disciples about the kingdom. He preached, "Repent, for the kingdom of Heaven is near" (Matt 3:2; 4:17). The beatitudes begin and end with illustrations of the present availability of the kingdom (Matt 5:3, 10), thus "framing the collection of Beatitudes (an inclusion) and suggesting that they must be understood within its thought compass."[13] In fact, Willard believes that the beatitudes are really a kingdom proclamation. For him, "they serve to clarify Jesus' fundamental message: the free availability of God's rule and righteousness to all of humanity through reliance upon Jesus himself, the person now loose in the world among us."[14] By illustrating the kingdom heart of love in the rest of the Sermon on the Mount, Jesus showed that it is virtually impossible to do the things described without being substantially transformed from the inside out. By contrasting kingdom righteousness with the righteousness of the Pharisees and teachers of the law (Matt 6:19–20), Jesus reveals their mistake: "The Pharisee takes as his aim keeping the law rather than becoming the kind of person whose deeds naturally conform to the law."[15]

Jesus traveled around in order to proclaim the good news of the kingdom to more and more people (Luke 8:1). In fact, he insisted on moving to other cities in order to preach the good news of the kingdom there, even though the crowds would have preferred that he stayed (Luke 4:42–43). He instructed the disciples to preach the kingdom when he sent them out to minister (Matt 10:7; Luke 9:1–3; 10:9). The kingdom was so important to Jesus, because when people enter into the kingdom they become God's dance partners and take their place in the Father's dream of a radiant and glorious bride.

Jesus' vision for the kingdom of God to come to earth and redeem God's bride was the motivating factor behind his incarnation, life, ministry, and death on the cross. Knowing that he was demonstrating the kingdom life and sacrificing his life for the sake of the bride gave him tremendous joy and passion in his endeavors. Jesus saw a picture of a preferred future for humanity, and he resolutely determined to bring about that reality.

---

13. Green et al., eds., *Dictionary of Jesus and the Gospels*, s.vv. "The kingdom of heaven."

14. Willard, *Divine Conspiracy*, 116.

15. Ibid., 184.

Part 2: A Theology of the Trinitarian Leadership Dance

He imparted this vision to his disciples, and it so inspired and motivated them that they were transformed and were used to transform their world. Canadian leaders also must catch a glimpse of the kingdom of God that Christ has established here on earth. In so doing, they will overcome their Canadian reticence to speaking out on issues of truth and faith and become emboldened to speak the truth in love and become a more radiant bride. Their churches will become transformed into authentic communities that communicate hope to cynics and skeptics alike. Only by recapturing this vision will the Canadian church become transformed and be used to transform the nation.

The Holy Spirit's Vision: Each Person's Assignment

All vision must be a subset of God's grand vision. Throughout biblical history, the Holy Spirit communicated God's plan and purpose to his people through dreams and visions. Not having any visions is described in the Scripture as undesirable; it is a time of night or a time of mourning (Mic 3:6; 1 Sam 3:1; Lam 2:9). He spoke to the patriarchs Abraham (Gen 15:1) and Jacob (Gen 46:2) in a vision. Joseph was called a dreamer because God spoke to him through dreams (Gen 37:19). God used a vision to call Samuel into service (1 Sam 3:15). He revealed his will to the prophets through visions (Isa 1:1; Ezek 1:1; Dan 1:17; Obad 1:1; Mic 1:1; Nah 1:1; Zech 1:8; Hos 12:10). The Apostles Peter and Paul were redirected on their missionary travels by means of a vision (Acts 10:10–17; 16:6–9; 18:9; 26:19). The closing words of the Bible, the Book of Revelation, are God's vision of the future revealed to the Apostle John (Rev 9:17).

Leaders see a new reality long before others do. Martin Luther King Jr. inspired his followers with his famous "I Have a Dream" speech.[16] Sir John A. MacDonald envisioned a united nation with two diverse European colonial origins.[17] Pierre Elliot Trudeau dreamed of bringing the Charter of Rights and Freedoms to Canada.[18] Mahatma Gandhi had a vision of nonviolent resistance overcoming British rule and achieving an independent Indian state.[19] Nelson Mandela dreamed of a country free from apartheid.

---

16. King Jr., "I Have a Dream."
17. Johnson, "Sir John A. Macdonald."
18. Ibid., s.v. "Trudeau, Pierre Elliott."
19. Prabhu and Rao, eds., *Mind of Mahatma Gandhi*.

Mother Teresa envisioned the poor dying with dignity.[20] Billy Graham envisioned packed stadiums of people listening to the proclamation of the Gospel.[21]

Hybels pictured transforming irreligious people into totally dedicated followers of Jesus Christ. Gilbert Bilezikian, who painted such a compelling picture of the church that it still moves Hybels to tears, inspired him.[22] Those who are led by God have a transformative vision for a preferred future, for the Holy Spirit not only speaks to leaders but also to ordinary believers (Acts 9:10; 10:3). In fact, one of the characteristics of being filled with the Holy Spirit is the ability to see visions or to dream dreams (Joel 2:28; Acts 2:17).[23]

A clearly articulated description of the future, birthed in a leader's heart by the Holy Spirit, is the best compass for navigating the journey of participating in God's transformational mission. In order to discern God's vision, one need only ask and wait for a revelation (Hab 2:1; Jas 1:5). The disciplines of silence and solitude are helpful in waiting for God's vision. Once a vision is received, it is good to write it down so that it can be recalled whenever one is discouraged or the future seems hopeless (Hab 2:2–3). Discerning God's vision for one's unique situation will transform a disengaged Canadian church into one that is passionate about participating in God's transformational mission in this land and beyond.

DISCERNING SHARED VALUES

Values are "a set of core beliefs or standards in which an individual or a group has an emotional investment (either for or against)."[24] They are important, because values reveal what individuals and groups actually believe deep in their hearts. An exploration of the interdynamics displayed among the members of the Trinity provides a glimpse of God's values. While there are numerous values that the Trinity exhibits,[25] four significant ones stand

20. "Mother Teresa—Biographical."
21. "William (Billy) F. Graham."
22. Hybels, *Courageous Leadership*, 30.
23. *New Bible Dictionary*, s.v. "visions." According to this source, "the border-line between vision and dream and trance is difficult, if not impossible to determine."
24. *Dictionary.com*, s.v. "values."
25. Johnson, *Experiencing the Trinity*, 77–84, lists the following values: intimacy, joy, servanthood, purity, power, creativity, and peace. Gruenler, *Trinity in the Gospel of John*,

out as important for the leadership dance: mutuality, equality, relational focus, and joy. These values are essential for leaders who wish to emulate the Trinity's dance of love and life in their local context.

Mutuality

Since each member of the Trinity is bound intimately within the life of the others, there is a mutuality of love among all three members and a mutual submission to one another. There is reciprocal admiration and respect for one another, resulting in mutual deference to one another. The Father loves the Son and declares at his baptism, "You are my Son, whom I love; with you I am well pleased" (Luke 3:22), and places on the Son his "seal of approval" (John 6:27). He respects him so much that he "has placed everything in his hands" (John 3:35), "shows him all he does" (John 5:20), shares with him "all that belongs to the Father" (John 16:15), and even grants him "all authority in heaven and on earth" (Matt 28:18). The Father does not view himself as superior or the Son as inferior; rather, he grants the Son the same divine status as himself.

Moreover, the Father respects the Spirit, gives him as a good gift without limit to all who ask (Luke 11:13; John 3:34), declares that "God is spirit" (John 4:23), and insists that "the Father be worshipped in Spirit and in truth" (John 4:23–24). God the Father also defers to the Spirit by submitting to the Spirit residing in believers when they call out to him in prayer.[26] Those to whom Jesus promises the Holy Spirit in John 14, he also promises to "give whatever you [believers] ask in . . . [his] name" (John 15:16; 16:23–26). The Spirit is not viewed as a junior partner in the Trinity; instead, he is respected as an equal member of the divine Godhead.

Jesus loves the Father so much that he submits to his wisdom and will. Jesus yields to the Father's will by being born in human likeness (Phil 2:7), by doing "only what he sees his Father doing" (John 5:19), by not speaking

---

v, 1–140, identifies the social nature, family, community, and being one. Seamand, *Ministry in the Image of God*, 1–178, suggests relational personhood, joyful intimacy, glad surrender, complex simplicity, gracious self-acceptance, mutual indwelling, and passionate mission. Cladis, *Leading the Team-Based Church*, 33–154, recognizes covenanting, visionary, culture creating, collaborative, trusting, empowering, and learning.

26. Those who hold a monarchian view of the Trinity may differ in their understanding of the mutuality between the Father and the Spirit. Ratzinger, *Church, Ecumenism, and Politics*, 29–62; see also Volf, *After our Likeness*, 29–72; and Buxton, *Trinity, Creation and Pastoral Ministry*, 154.

of his own accord but "only what the Father commands him to say" (John 12:49–50), and especially by his death on the cross (Matt 26:39; Phil 2:8). He understands the assignment that his Father has given to him (Luke 22:42; John 5:17, 22), seeks only the Father's will (John 6:40; Luke 22:42), and completes the work that his Father sent him to do (John 5:36; 19:30). He asks the Father, before sending the Spirit (John 14:16), and the Father consults with the Son prior to sending the Spirit in Jesus' name (John 14:26). Jesus did not consider equality with God something that de facto made his decisions final (Phil 2:6). He always consulted and submitted to the Father, just as the Father also consulted and mutually submitted to the Spirit and to the Son.

Jesus surrenders to the Spirit and allows the Spirit to fill him even from birth (Luke 1:15), to lead him into the desert to be tempted (Matt 4:11), and to perform miracles through him (Luke 4:14, 18). He esteems the Holy Spirit so highly that he is eager to protect him and asserts, "Anyone who speaks a word against the Son of Man will be forgiven, but anyone who speaks against the Holy Spirit will not be forgiven, either in this age or in the age to come" (Matt 12:32). He recognizes that his life is intimately bound up in the life of the Spirit by announcing at the beginning of his ministry, "The Spirit of the Lord is on me" (Luke 4:18). There is a reciprocal relationship of mutual love, respect, and submission between the Spirit and the Son.

The Spirit also admires the Son, descending on him like a dove at his baptism (Mark 1:10), filling him with power (Luke 4:14, 18), and testifying only about Jesus (John 15:26). Both the Father and the Son send the Spirit, which reveals both their admiration and trust in the Holy Spirit and the Spirit's submission to be sent by them (John 14:26; 15:26). As well, the Holy Spirit defers to the wisdom of the Father by not speaking on his own; rather, he says "only what he hears" and tells "what is yet to come" (John 16:13). The Spirit submits to the Father's voice and only communicates what the Father wills. The Spirit has no inferiority complex but seeks only to bring glory to the Son (John 15:14).

These passages reveal that each person of the Trinity defers to, honors, and respects the others. Canadian theologian Clark H. Pinnock contends, "Loving mutuality and relationship belong to the essence of God."[27] There is a genuine spirit of humility in attitude and in action toward one another in a perichoretic understanding of the Trinity. Each one consults with, sub-

---

27. Pinnock, *Flame of Love*, 47.

mits to, and acts in partnership with the others. No unilateral decisions or actions are ever made; each member of the Trinity mutually relies on the wisdom, guidance, and strength of one another. Leupp observes, "There are no social climbers or influence peddlers in the Trinity. There is only grace, benediction, and beatitude."[28] What emerges from this value of mutuality is a real oneness of essence and of action.

Equality

Equality among the three members of the triune God is another fundamental value that the triune Godhead displays. The Jews tried to kill Jesus because he claimed equal status with God by calling him Father (John 5:18). The writer of Hebrews argues that Jesus Christ is the "exact representation" of God's being (Heb 1:3). Even before a full-fledged doctrine of the Trinity was developed, the Apostle Paul considered all three persons of the Trinity to be equal, even placing the grace of Christ before the love of God in his trinitarian blessing (2 Cor 13:14). Jesus commanded his disciples to baptize people in the name of the Father and of the Son and of the Holy Spirit, which indicates that each person enjoyed equal status (Matt 28:19).

Not all theologians have espoused this. A contrary perspective, called the subordinationist view, claims that there is an eternal and hierarchical relationship between the Father and the Son, which also extends to the Spirit. However, in contemporary discussions, Protestant, Roman Catholic, and Eastern Orthodox theologians alike all have come to agree that the three persons of the Trinity are "reciprocally related: none is before or after another, none is less or greater than another, none is subordinated in being or function to another."[29] Kevin Giles conclusively argues that while the New Testament can be read to support either view, the historically orthodox understanding is found in the latter view: the three persons of the Trinity are coequal and coeternal.[30]

From such an understanding of equality within the Godhead, believers are called in their interpersonal relationships "to function in a relationship of equality, of mutual respect, in which we understand that others are as important to God as we are, and treat them as equals."[31] Paul expands on

---

28. Leupp, *Knowing the Name of God*, 165.
29. Giles, *Trinity and Subordinationism*, 21.
30. Ibid., 25.
31. Erickson, *Making Sense of the Trinity*, 90.

this value of equality when he describes individual Christians as members of the Body of Christ (1 Cor 12), with "equal concern" for one another (1 Cor 12:25). Going farther, he declares that "there is neither Jew nor Greek, slave nor free, male nor female" (Gal 3:28), because all are "one in Christ Jesus" (Gal 3:28).

Relational

The third value that is reflected by the triune God is the value of being relationally focused. The early church understood that what was fundamental about God was the Trinity. The intimate connectivity among the Father, Son, and Spirit captured their hearts and imaginations. The mere fact that the Son stepped down into humanity in the incarnation for the purpose of relating to the human race was awesome and compelling. In referring to the Trinity, Johnson affirms that "at the center of the universe is a relationship."[32]

However, many people in the Canadian church have no personal relationship with God. They assume that God is remote and distant from everyday life. Kruger argues that the Western portrayal of Jesus as "paying the penalty for sin" has "eclipsed the incarnation" and "downsized" Jesus into a mere "spectator" in the universe.[33] Jesus came to earth in order to share the love that he experienced in his relationship with the Father with humanity, so that they also would experience this love in relationship with God and with one another (John 17:26). Pinnock agrees and states, "Let God not be defined so much by holiness and sovereignty in which loving relatedness is incidental, but by the dance of trinitarian life."[34] Intimate relationships naturally bring joy to life, a smile to one's face, comfort to the soul, and peace to the anxious heart. Similarly, Canadian leaders must be focused relationally when battling a privatized culture and an individualized faith.

Joy

The fourth value reflected by the Trinity is joy. Leupp suggests that all of God's activity results from his joy, saying, "Divine joy empowers the divine

---

32. Johnson, *Experiencing the Trinity*, 37.
33. Kruger, *Great Dance*, 29.
34. Pinnock, *Flame of Love*, 47.

dance."³⁵ Joy goes beyond happiness, for it is found not only in happy circumstances but also in connection to obedience to the divine will as evidenced by Paul and Silas's rejoicing even when they were in prison (Acts 16:25). Joy is expressed as a deep sense of delight, celebration, even ecstasy. It is experienced when one marries the person of his or her dreams, when one hears the cry of a newborn baby, when a son or daughter graduates, or one accomplishes one's dream after persevering trial after trial. It is expressed in deep and meaningful conversations and relationships. It is enjoyed by obedience to God's vision. By following the Holy Spirit's leading and guidance, Canadian Christians can experience great joy. In fact, Pinnock suggests that the Holy Spirit has a unique contribution to a sense of joy treasured by the members of the Trinity. He writes, "Spirit is the ecstasy of divine life, the overabundance of joy that gives birth to the universe and ever works to bring about a fullness of unity."³⁶

Perichoresis is the ultimate expression of joy and ecstasy. The deep, loving, and caring relationship among the three persons of the Trinity is one of mutual delight, celebration, and rejoicing. Each marvels and enjoys the other. Johnson describes this joy in the following way: "God really enjoys being God! The Father enjoys the Son: 'You are my constant delight.' And the Son enjoys the Father: 'In you does my soul rejoice.' And that joy is so real that it is embodied in the Holy Spirit."³⁷ The intimacy experienced by such interpenetration is perhaps an ecstasy reserved only for divine beings, for as Volf explains, "In a strict sense, there can be no correspondence to the interiority of the divine persons at the human level."³⁸ When humans experience joy, they taste a morsel of this divine ecstasy and delight that is enjoyed by the Father, Spirit, and Son.

When Lewis discovered God, he was shocked to realize that joy and God were connected. He did not even suspect that there was a relationship between God and joy; it just never had occurred to him.³⁹ Like Lewis, many Canadians would not equate God with joy. Kruger attributes this loss of joy in the Western understanding of God as a shift in understanding about the fundamental nature of God. The early church knew that the fundamental nature of God was the Trinity. In the development of Western theology, the

---

35. Leupp, *Knowing the Name of God*, 162.
36. Pinnock, *Flame of Love*, 48.
37. Johnson, *Experiencing the Trinity*, 78–79.
38. Volf, *After Our Likeness*, 210.
39. Lewis, *Surprised by Joy*, 16.

holiness of God was substituted for the Trinity as the basic truth about God, but it was a deficient view of holiness. Kruger explains, "For the holiness of God, properly understood, is simply beautiful. If we took the joy and the fullness and the love of the Father, Son and Spirit, their mutual delight and passion, the sheer togetherness of their relationship, its intimacy, harmony and wholeness and rolled them all into one word, it would be 'holiness.'"[40] Celebration, passion, and fun are exactly what must be recovered in the Canadian church today in order to restore a spirit of joy that is reflected in the life of the Trinity.

The four values central to the nature and being of *perichoresis*—mutuality, equality, relationship, and joy—are essential to the leadership dance. The goal of Christian leadership is to participate in the loving fellowship of the Trinity, inviting others and bringing in as many as possible into this eternal dance of love. Boyd contends, "God's desire for us is to participate in his own eternal love and life and therefore in his own joy and peace by dwelling in the Son. We are to dance with the Father, Son, and Holy Spirit in the joyful celebration of their eternal love and life."[41] Leaders must embrace these trinitarian values and model them in their lives and with their teams in order to learn the leadership dance without stepping on toes.

DEVELOPING COLLABORATIVE STRATEGY

God's strategic plan for establishing the kingdom can be seen in the acts of creation, redemption, and sanctification. The Godhead experiences such joy and delight that humanity is created in his image so that they might share in this divine joy. When humanity fell, the Trinity reached out in redemption to bring them back into the circle of the dance, so they could experience the joy and delight in a relationship with God and with one another once again (1 John 1:3–4). Torrance explains, "God draws near to us in such a way as to draw us near to himself within the circle of his knowing of himself."[42] As human beings struggle with the pain and sorrow of sin and brokenness in the world, the Trinity empowers and sanctifies them to become increasingly transformed into the image of the Son and one day to become God's beautiful bride. All three members of the Trinity act in concert to orchestrate this plan, however, one member is central to each

40. Kruger, *Great Dance*, 30.
41. Boyd, *Repenting of Religion*, 15.
42. Torrance, *Trinitarian Perspectives*, 2.

part. The Father creates the world and humanity in order to share his dance of love with them. The Son redeems people in order to bring them back into the dance of relationship. The Spirit indwells and transforms believers, helping them dance with the Father, day by day. These three events—creation, redemption, and sanctification—reflect God's strategic plan for accomplishing his vision and his dream of a pure and spotless bride.

Creation

The first part of God's strategy is creation. The Bible teaches that the universe, including all matter, came into existence through the will of the Creator (Gen 1–2; Heb 11:3). By his wisdom, he created the heavens and the earth (Gen 1–2, Ps 96:5; Isa 37:16). All of creation glorifies him (Ps 19:1) by obeying his plan and carrying out his will. He designed humankind to care for and steward his creation (Gen 1:26, 28). He shapes individuals in the womb (Isa 44:24), knows every detail of each person's life (Ps 139), and calls each one by name (Isa 43:1). He challenges any who disagree with his plan, presenting his acts of creation as evidence of his good judgment (Isa 45: 9–12). Likewise, he defies any other deity's power, using the display of his creation as proof of his superior power and greatness (Jer 10:11–12).

While the Father did not need to create, he did so according to his good pleasure for his plan and purpose. Creation was born of love—the same love with which the Father loves the Son.[43] The very process of creating the world is "identified with the inner-trinitarian life."[44] God's freedom to create, according to Jürgen Moltmann, is synonymous with God's freedom to love: "out of freedom" means "out of love."[45] Consequently, there is a reciprocal relationship between the world and God. "Creation is the fruit of God's longing for his Other and for the Other's free response to the divine love. That is why the idea of the world is inherent in the nature of God himself from eternity."[46] Creation reflects the very heart and nature of God, because it is an expression of the Trinity's creative power and the kingdom of God. It is small wonder, then, that people often experience God's presence when they experience nature, for as Willard describes, they are "skin

---

43. Moltmann, *Trinity and the Kingdom*, 106–8, 111–12.
44. Ibid., 107–8.
45. Moltmann, *God in Creation*, 75–76.
46. Moltmann, *Trinity and the Kingdom*, 138.

to skin" with God's kingdom.[47] The Creator values creation, because it is an extension of himself and his creative spirit. The Father also values humanity, calling people the crowning achievement of all creation (Ps 8).

Buxton argues that "relationality," suggested by *perichoresis*, is an essential dimension of God's imprint on creation. All that is in the universe is bound up with everything else. Since God is involved intimately with his creation, "his perichoretic life spills over into everything 'other' that he has brought into being."[48] He argues that *perichoresis* conveys a dynamic vitality of God, who is "immanently involved in his creation and whose life in the history of the world is constitutive of his essential being *ad intra*."[49] He shows how interconnectedness, coherence, holism, and harmony—words that suggest *perichoresis*—are themes that emerge from new scientific discoveries. The physical universe is an integrated and interconnected reality that images the Trinity who has brought this world into being and sustains it by his Spirit. By examining key topics in contemporary physics, such as quantum mechanics, chaos and complexity, emergence and self-organization, Buxton concludes that God's perichoretic life is present and represented in all of creation.[50]

Redemption

The second part of the Trinity's strategy is to redeem fallen humanity. Jesus' purpose was clear right from his birth (Matt 2:11; Luke 2:29–32). He knew that he was to lay down his life willingly (John 10:11). He told his disciples three times that he had to suffer and die (Matt 16:21; 20:17; 26:2). Despite incredible pain, Jesus considered the final outcome worth the cost of his earthy life (Luke 22:42; Heb 12:2). As a result, he took the penalty for sin by dying on a cross (Isa 53:5) and making redemption possible through his blood (Rom 3:24; Heb 9:12).

According to Moltmann, redemption is central to an understanding of the Trinity and belongs to the inner life of God. He argues, "The cross of the Son stands from eternity in the center of the Trinity,"[51] such that God is revealed in the suffering and shame of the cross. Therefore, he argues that

---

47. Willard with Matthews, "Spirituality and Ministry."
48. Buxton, *Trinity, Creation, and Pastoral Ministry*, 195.
49. Ibid., 205.
50. Buxton, *Trinity, Creation, and Pastoral Ministry*, 195–245.
51. Moltmann, *Trinity and the Kingdom*, xvi, 78.

what happened on the cross was not an event between God and humanity but between God and God: "It was a deep division in God himself, in so far as God abandoned God and contradicted himself, and at the same time a unity in God, in so far as God was at one with God and corresponded to himself."[52] In the crucifixion the Son suffers the pain of being cut off from the Father, and the Father suffers grief in the giving up of his Son. In *The Crucified God*, rather than focusing solely on the suffering "of" God, Moltmann also highlights the suffering "in" God. From his perspective, this inter-trinitarian dynamic is what moves the plan of redemption "from the exterior of the mystery which is called 'God' to the interior, which is trinitarian."[53]

Sanctification

The third part of God's strategy in accomplishing his vision is sanctification. The Scripture teaches that before the creation of the world God chose believers to be holy and blameless in his sight (Eph 1:4). This process occurs as the Holy Spirit works God's character into the life of the believer. As believers are filled with the Holy Spirit (Eph 5:18), they experience the divine life flowing in and through them. The result is love, joy, peace, patience, kindness, goodness, faithfulness, gentleness, and self-control (Gal 5:22–23). When believers listen to the voice of the Holy Spirit and obey his Word (John 14:15), they are filled with inexplicable joy knowing that God has chosen them to fulfill his plans. The Holy Spirit also reveals that they are no longer orphans but adopted into God's family (John 14:18). Consequently, by the Holy Spirit, they cry, "Abba Father" (Rom 8:15; Gal 4:6) and experience his power, love, and self-discipline in their ordinary, everyday lives (2 Tim 1:7).

Since the Father and Son are in one another and Christians are in them (John 17:21), humans are able to experience "a type" of unity that the Father, Son, and Spirit experience. It is only "a type" of unity, since humanity cannot completely experience interpenetration as the Godhead does.[54] However, the degree to which humans experience and reflect the mutual love, sharing, delight, and compassion of the Father, Son, and Spirit is the degree to which they are sanctified. As the Holy Spirit works in the Cana-

---

52. Moltmann, *Crucified God*, 244.
53. Ibid., 204.
54. Volf, *After Our Likeness*, 210.

Movement II: Choreography

dian church to sanctify it, making believers one, it increasingly will become the radiant, resplendent, and lustrous bride of the Father's desire.

Vision, values, and strategy are the three steps that choreograph God's plan and purposes. Embracing these purposes, leaders join together with the Trinity in the dance of participating in that which God is already doing here on earth. Knowing God's plan, believers unite, under the inspiration of the Trinity, to announce Christ's second coming. Understanding these steps, leaders influence others to also join in God's plan. Nevertheless, providing these steps alone is insufficient for the dance of leaders. These plans must be orchestrated well in order to fully engage in the trinitarian leadership dance. This is the focus of the next movement: orchestration.

7

Movement III: Orchestration

The third movement of the Trinitarian Dance is orchestration and involves two-way communication, conflict resolution, and forgiveness. To execute one's strategy, a leader must possess excellent communication skills. Change often leads to conflict, so transformational leaders need resolution skills to bring about God's vision. Reflecting the heart of the Trinity, leaders must exercise a great deal of forgiveness, for loving often involves pain. Lack of forgiveness can sidetrack leaders with bitterness, envy, and resentment and stop the flow of the Trinitarian Dance of love and life within them. Two-way communication, conflict resolution, and forgiveness are the steps needed to orchestrate God's divine initiatives, participating in God's transformative mission here on earth.

PRACTICING TWO-WAY COMMUNICATION

Two-way communication is the first step in the orchestration of any vision. Communication is the transmission of a message from a sender to a receiver. A message is encoded by the sender and decoded by the receiver, both of whom have filters that might block or distort sending or receiving the message. By stating that communication is the transmitting of messages from speaker to listener, this implies that the process begins with the speaker and ends with the listener. In reality, however, interpersonal communication is circular. Each person is simultaneously a speaker and a listener. This circular dance of sending and receiving messages is what is meant by two-way communication. The leaders cast vision, receive input, clarify expectations, and revise plans based on other people's feedback and the actual situation in the organization.

This type of communication stands in contrast to one-way communication, where leaders simply tell others what to do or try to win or persuade the rest of the group to their point of view. Herrington, Bonem, and Furr describe the difference by distinguishing between dialog (two-way communication) and discussion (one-way communication): "The purpose of dialog is to go beyond any one individual's understanding. In dialog, each individual's understanding is made available to the entire group so that all learn. In discussion, an individual's perspective on an issue is presented with the objective of persuading the rest of the group."[1]

Not surprisingly, the Trinity eschews one-way communication in favor of dialog or two-way communication. Each member of the Godhead displays this type of respectful dialog with one another. The very notion of *perichoresis* is the idea that there is mutual indwelling yet distinction within the Trinity. The conversation between Father, Son, and Holy Spirit is one that is similar to all relationships: interactive, dynamic, and responsive. The mutuality and equality among Father, Spirit, and Son ensures this type of open exchange and dialog. Moreover, God himself engages in two-way communication with his people.

Yahweh: The God Who Speaks and Hears

Throughout the pages of Scripture God speaks to his people. In the beginning, God spoke and all of creation came into being (Gen 1). He walked with Adam and Eve in the garden (Gen 2). He instructed Noah to build an ark to save his family and two of every kind of animal from the coming destruction (Gen 6:13–21). He called Abram and instructed him to leave his country and go to another land (Gen 12:1–4). God spoke to Jacob in a dream (Gen 28:13) and wrestled with him (Gen 32:22–32). He even spoke to the pagan Pharaoh of Egypt through dreams and revealed the interpretation to Joseph (Gen 41:1–40). In the burning bush, God revealed himself to Moses as the eternal "I Am" (Exod 3:14) and continued to speak with him face to face, as a friend (Exod 33:11). He spoke the Ten Commandments (Exod 20:1) and gave his laws to his people (Ps 147:19). Throughout Israel's history, God disclosed his will, exhorted, admonished, and warned

1. Herrington et al., *Leading Congregational Change*, 140–42.

his people through the prophets. God has not been silent or absent from his creation but has been intensely present in all of history and all of life.

Not only does God speak, God also listens and remembers. God took notice of Sarah's maidservant, Hagar, when she cried out to him in prayer (Gen 16:11; 17: 20). God heard the Israelites groaning and was concerned about them (Exod 2:24). He paid attention to the Israelites grumbling and complaining in the wilderness (Exod 16: 7–9). When Moses petitioned the Almighty regarding the impending calamity that was to come upon the Israelites, God relented and did not bring the disaster that he had threatened (Exod 32:14). In addition, he withdrew the swarm of locusts and judgment by fire from the Israelites when the prophet Amos cried out to him (Amos 7:1–6). The Scripture reminds us that the prayers of the righteous are powerful and effective (Jas 5:16), meaning that God listens and responds to his chosen ones when they appeal to him through prayer.

Jesus Christ: The Word of God

God spoke his ultimate Word when Jesus became a man and walked on the earth (John 1:14; Heb 1:1–2). Jesus is referred to as the "Word of God" (John 1:1) and the exact representation of God's being (Heb 1:3). He reflected God's glory and communicated God's grace and truth (Heb 1:3; John 1:17). John explains, "No one has ever seen God, but God, the One and Only, who is at the Father's side, has made him known" (John 1:18).

Jesus was in constant communion and communication with the Father and the Spirit while he walked here on earth. He declared that it was possible to listen and to learn from the Father (John 6:45). He spoke only what the Father taught him (John 8:28) and only what he had seen in the Father's presence (John 8:38). Jesus did not teach on his own but taught only what the Father instructed him (John 7:16). He always was doing the will of his Father by the power of the Holy Spirit (John 6:38). Even when there was a seeming contradiction between the will of the Father and Christ's desire, Jesus felt comfortable communicating his heart's desire to the Father by crying out, "My Father, if it is possible, may this cup be taken from me" (Matt 26:39a). The Father felt equally comfortable to remind the Son of the necessity of the cross to redeem the world, such that the Son conceded, "Not my will, but yours be done" (Matt 26:39b).

Jesus' communication with the Father did not flow simply in one direction, for the Father also listened to the Son. Jesus asked the Father for certain prayer requests on behalf of the disciples (John 14:16; 17:1–26). Jesus declared that the Father always heard him but spoke things aloud, at times, for the benefit of others (John 11:41–42). The Father confirmed this declaration by speaking aloud as well (John 12:30). Two-way communication between the Father and the Son was the only type of communication their relationship of mutuality and equality understood.

Not only did Jesus communicate with the Father, he also communicated with his disciples and with the crowds. He spoke to his disciples and called them to follow him (Luke 5:1–11). He announced the reality of the kingdom of heaven and invited all to repent and believe the good news (Matt 4:17). He communicated through parables and stories and took advantage of teachable moments to drive home his message. He spoke figuratively at times but also instructed plainly and clearly at other times (John 16:25). L. Ford observes, "He [Jesus] was able to create, articulate and communicate a compelling vision; to change what people talk about and dream of; to make his followers transcend self interest; to enable us to see ourselves and our world in a new way; to provide prophetic insight into the very heart of things; and to bring about the highest order of change."[2] He spoke with love and respect towards all who approached him, including tax collectors and sinners (Matt 9:10–11; Mark 2:15–16; Luke 15:1; Luke 7:36–37). One can only imagine Jesus choosing a respectful dialog between equals as his preferred mode of communication.

The Holy Spirit Communicates

God still communicates with believers today through the Holy Spirit. The Holy Spirit is described as someone who will teach believers all things and remind them of everything Jesus taught (John 14:26). Like the Son, the Holy Spirit does not speak on his own but only says what he hears from the Father and the Son (John 16:13). He will guide believers in what to say in their moment of trial (Luke 12:12). After Jesus rose from the grave, he gave instructions to the disciples through the Holy Spirit (Acts 1:2). Jesus declared that his sheep listen for, hear, and know his voice (John 10:3–4, 15). They will not follow a stranger, because they do not recognize a stranger's voice (John 10:5). In fact, Scripture warns against hardening one's heart against the voice of the Holy Spirit (Heb 3:7–8). God desires not only to communicate with believers but to be intimately involved in every facet of

2. Ford, *Transforming Leadership*, 15.

Part 2: A Theology of the Trinitarian Leadership Dance

a believer's life. Willard points out, "Hearing God is but one dimension of a richly interactive relationship, and obtaining guidance is but one facet of hearing God."[3]

God also speaks through the Bible, which was inspired by the Holy Spirit. The Holy Spirit superintended the human writers in the production of the Scriptures so that what they wrote was precisely what God wanted written (2 Pet 1:21; 2 Tim 3:16). The Spirit showed God's revelation to the Apostle John on the Island of Patmos (Rev 1:10; 21:10). All the prophets were led by God's Holy Spirit when they predicted the coming Messiah (1 Pet 1:10–12). God promised protection and healing for all those who obeyed his voice by following his decrees (Exod 15:25–27). Christian leaders, therefore, must become completely familiar with God's Word.

While God's thoughts are not human (Isa 55:8), the Bible makes it clear that God's voice is discernable. Whether in a still small voice (1 Kgs 19:11–12) or marvelous thunder (Job 37:5; 40:9; Ps 29:3), God's Word has the effect of piercing the soul (Heb 4:12) like fire or a hammer (Jer 23:29). Those who belong to God hear God's voice (John 8:47). Believers ought to take time to communicate with the lover of their soul, as Christ has opened up the way for this communication to take place.

Throughout the New Testament, the Holy Spirit was very active in the church and the lives of individual believers. The Holy Spirit inspired Peter to give a defense before the Sadducees of how the crippled beggar was healed (Acts 4:8). Likewise, the Holy Spirit encouraged the early church (Acts 9:31) and directed them to set apart Barnabas and Saul for the missionary journeys that God inspired (Acts 13:2). The Holy Spirit guided these missionary journeys, preventing them from traveling in Asia, but opening doors for them to preach in Phrygia, Galatia, and Macedonia (Acts 16:6). The Spirit also led Philip in the conversion of the Ethiopian eunuch and his preaching in the towns in Judea (Acts 8:26–40). Once believers were filled with the Holy Spirit, they were empowered to speak God's word boldly (Acts 4:31). Perhaps a lack of communication with the Holy Spirit today is the cause of much of the dispassionate expression of faith in Canada.

RESOLVING CONFLICT

Not only must leaders communicate well, they must be able to resolve conflict. Reggie McNeal affirms, "The decision to serve as a spiritual leader

---

3. Willard, *Hearing God*, 10.

signs one up for conflict."[4] Most biblical characters encountered conflict as they followed God. Moses battled with Pharaoh over God's will for his people. Even within his own leadership team, Moses encountered difficulties (Num 12:2). Joseph experienced conflict within his family (Gen 37) and, despite his innocence, with Potiphar's wife (Gen 39). These conflicts shaped his character and prepared him to become second in command of all of Egypt (Gen 41:41). King David fought many wars before and after ascending to the throne. These conflicts also shaped his character and revealed his deep understanding of God's sovereignty in appointing leaders (1 Sam 24:10). Even before being sent to prophesy, Isaiah was warned that the people would not follow his leadership easily but would ignore his words and harden their hearts (Isa 6:9–10). The Apostle Paul did not mince words when he spoke against the Judaizers, who were constantly at odds with kingdom principles (Gal 5:12). In fact, the Scriptures make it very clear that those who want to lead a godly life will be persecuted (2 Tim 3:12). Therefore, spiritual leaders must master how to handle conflict by understanding that God is the one who protects, defends, and fights for his servants.

The three persons of the Trinity dance in perfect harmony and unison in the eternal dance of love and life. However, since Christ now has opened up the dance to a new partner—humanity—this new partner is often "out of step" with the dance. Some leaders are ignorant of the dance or are still learning the steps. These missteps create tension and conflict, not within the Trinity, but between God's vision and current reality.

God, the Creator

While the Trinity exists in perfect unity, God's creation and his creatures are not yet perfectly united with their Creator. Since the fall, humanity has been in constant conflict and rebellion with God. Cain murdered Abel in direct opposition to God's plan. Humanity became so corrupt that the Lord wanted to wipe humankind from the face of the earth by sending the flood (Gen 6:7). Similarly, when the Israelites grumbled against the Lord, he was ready to destroy them with a plague and start over with Moses and his descendants (Num 14:11–12). The entire Bible is the story of God's fight against his enemies and his ultimate triumph over them.

---

4. McNeal, *Work of Heart*, 155.

Part 2: A Theology of the Trinitarian Leadership Dance

In the midst of the fray, God promises to be a protector, shield, and strong fortress to all who align themselves with him (Ps 91). He fights for his people and is an enemy to their enemies (Exod 23: 22). He promises victory for the righteous (Lev 26:7–8). In fact, one of God's names is *Jehovah Tsabaoth*, or the "Lord of the Armies" (1 Sam 17:45).[5] He is called a refuge, a rock, and a strong deliverer (2 Sam 22:2; Pss 18:2; 28:8; 31:2–3; 59:16). He is the Good Shepherd who not only guides and protects but also justifies his servants in front of their enemies (Ps 23). Christian leaders can trust in God's deliverance, protection, and ultimate victory as they seek to participate in what God is already doing here on earth (Ps 60:12).

Jesus Christ, the Son of God

God's kingdom came into sharp conflict with the kingdom of this world when Jesus became incarnate as a man. Unlike those belonging to the world's system, Jesus demonstrated that God's kingdom is not a matter of eating and drinking but of righteousness, peace, and joy in the Holy Spirit (Rom 14:17). He revealed that God's kingdom is not a matter of eloquent talking but of power (1 Cor 4:20). Jesus stepped into creation to battle and defeat God's enemies. Demons shrieked when Jesus invaded their territory (Mark 5:7). He clashed with the religious officials, calling them hypocrites (Matt 15:7–9), and had nothing good to say about them (Matt 12:34; 23). When he rose from the dead, he triumphed over his foes and made a public spectacle of them (Col 2:15).

Believers are to be encouraged by Jesus' faithful example, for he endured a great deal of opposition from sinful men (Heb 12:3). God vindicates his servants warning that it is his prerogative alone to avenge (Deut 32:35). Believers are instructed not to repay evil with evil but to trust in God's vengeance (1 Pet 3:9; Rom 12:17–19). As far as it depends on believers, we are to live at peace with everyone (Rom 12:18). However, as children of the light who shine on the dark deeds of the world, believers inevitably will clash with those who walk in darkness (Eph 5:8–11; John 3:19–20). It is during these times of conflict that Christian leaders must remember Christ's struggle and victory over the dark forces of evil (Heb 12:1–4; 1 Cor 15:58). Through Christ, believers have the final victory despite conflict, temptation, trials, and tribulations (1 Cor 15:57).

5. BDB, s.v. "tsaba."

Movement III: Orchestration

The Holy Spirit

The Holy Spirit is at the forefront of the war against the forces that oppose God's will, for the Holy Spirit was the agent through which Christ came into the world. The Holy Spirit overshadowed Mary, protected her, and effected God's will (Luke 1:35). The Spirit is the one who led Jesus into the desert to be tempted by the devil and also gave him strength to overcome those temptations (Luke 4:1–3). The Holy Spirit was the power that raised Christ from the dead and gave him ultimate victory over sin, hell, and the grave (Eph 1:19–20).

Those who follow God find themselves under direct attack from the world, the flesh, and the devil. Believers wrestle not against flesh and blood but against rulers, principalities, and spiritual forces of evil in the heavenly realms (Eph 6:12). Through the Spirit, believers are set free from the law of sin and death (Rom 8:2). By the Spirit, believers can experience the safety and security of God's kingdom, despite the conflicts and tribulations in this world. Through the Holy Spirit, believers have victory over the allure of the world (1 John 5:4). The Holy Spirit even brings victory over the grave to all who trust in Christ (1 Cor 15:54).

OFFERING FORGIVENESS

As leaders discern God's vision and plan within their specific context, they reflect God's heart and attributes. Forgiveness is one of the attributes that Christian leaders will be required to excel in when they encounter resistance to change and opposition to God's transformative vision. Walter C. Wright remarks, "When God calls us to leadership . . . that call includes forgiveness. I do not believe there can be leadership without forgiveness."[6] Forgiveness is necessary, because moving in a transformative direction will produce conflict as individuals express their reticence to change.

God, the Judge

One of God's names in the Old Testament is *Shaphat*, which is "God, the Judge"[7] (Gen 18:25; Judg 11:27; Job 9:15). Daniel's name literally means

---

6. Wright, *Relational Leadership*, 199.
7. BDB, s.v. "shaphat."

Part 2: A Theology of the Trinitarian Leadership Dance

"God is my Judge,"[8] constantly reminding the Israelites of God's judgment on them. In the New Testament, God is referred to as the judge of the living and the dead (Acts 10:42), the one who judges justly (1 Pet 2:23), and the only Lawgiver and Judge (Jas 4:12). He is depicted in the Revelation as the one seated on the throne, having authority to judge (Rev 20:4, 11). His judgments are righteous and just (Isa 11:4; Jer 11:20, Ezek 33:20). He judges between individuals (Ezek 34:17, 20, 22) and nations (Joel 3:12; Mic 4:3). Administering justice is one of God's attributes. In other words, as the just judge, God condemns and punishes injustice and sin. However, since God is also merciful, he does not want to punish sinners. So, there is a dilemma. On the one hand, the Judge must mete out punishment; on the other, the Good Shepherd has compassion for his lost sheep. God solved this dilemma by banging the gavel and declaring the sin contemptible, wrong, and deserving of punishment, and then stepping away from the bench and into the convict's chair to accept the death penalty for the crime. This is what God did when he sent his son Jesus to pay the penalty for sin (1 John 2:2; 4:10). Volf summarizes, "The world is sinful. That's why God doesn't affirm it indiscriminately. God loves the world. That's why God doesn't punish it in justice. What does God do with this double bind? God forgives."[9]

Scripture uses a number of metaphors to describe what God does with sin. God "covers" sin (Ps 32:1; Rom 4:7). Like a firefighter rescuing one caught in the flames, God takes the blanket of forgiveness and smothers them so that one can begin healing. God "blots out" sin (Isa 43:25; Ps 51:1, 9). Like the mother who blots the stain on her daughter's new white blouse, God soaks the stain of sin from his children's lives.

God "sweeps away our sin" like a "cloud" or a "morning mist" (Isa 44:22). Like the sunshine that dances on the leaves after the rain, God's favor rests on those whose sins have been forgiven. He "wipes out" sins (Acts 3:19) like a father wipes the mouth of his baby. God puts wrongdoing "behind his back" (Isa 38:17) and "hides his face" from iniquities (Ps 51:19). God looks at sinners but does not see the sin, because "one cannot see what's behind one's back."[10]

God "removes" offenses by putting them out of reach (Mic 7:19; Ps 103:12). Like a loving parent who cleans up after his messy children and puts away their toys, God cleans up sins and places them out of reach. God

---

8. *New Bible Dictionary*, s.v. "Daniel."
9. Miroslav Volf, *Free of Charge*, 140.
10. Ibid., 142.

"remembers sins no more" by putting them "out of his mind" (Isa 43:25; Jer 31:34; Heb 8:12; Heb 10:17). God does not forget, for he is omniscient; "to remember no more" means that judgment for the offense is removed and the matter is put out of mind. They simply are deleted from his memory banks. God does not "reckon sin" (Rom 4:8; Ps 32:1–2) against us. Volf elucidates, "We incur debt, but God puts nothing in the debit column of our life's account. We owe, but we don't have to pay."[11] He "cancels" the debt (Col 2:14), like a beneficent bank manager who deletes debt incurred by low-income families.

Jesus and the Cross

Jesus is the Lamb of God, who takes away the sins of the world (John 1:29). His very life was destined for the cross (Luke 2:34–35), which secured forgiveness for those who put their faith and trust in him. He resolutely set out to go to Jerusalem to accomplish the Father's will and to provide forgiveness for those who believe (Luke 9:51). He knew that his mission was to pay the penalty for sin, for he explained the necessity of his death three times to his disciples (Mark 8:31; 9:31; 10:33–34). He humbled himself to fulfill this mission and became obedient even unto death (Phil 2:8). His last words on the cross were these: "Father, forgive them for they do not know what they are doing" (Luke 23:34). Now, he is the atoning sacrifice, ready to forgive all who confess their sins and come to him in faith (1 John 1:9; 2:1). He is the Great High Priest who ever lives to intercede for those who go astray (Heb 4:14–16) and the Prince who gives forgiveness (Acts 5:31).

Christ instructed his disciples to forgive. He taught that forgiveness was as integral to the Christian life as prayer by including "forgive us our debts as we also have forgiven our debtors" in the Lord's Prayer (Matt 6:12). He warned of the danger of unforgiveness by avowing that if one does not forgive, one will not be forgiven (Matt 6:15). Once, Peter speculated that one should forgive more than twice what is prescribed by the Law. Jesus, however, surprised him by greatly exceeding that amount (Matt 18:21–22). On another occasion, when he instructed his disciples to forgive an unlimited amount each day, they objected and asked him to increase their faith (Luke 17:3–5). He replied by pointing out that faith as small as a mustard seed can move mountains (Luke 7:6). Then, he proceeded to tell the parable of the dutiful servant (Luke 17:7–10). It was as if he were saying that

11. Ibid.

a lack of forgiveness is not a "shortage of faith, but rather a shortage of obedience."[12] Dick Keyes summarizes, "Forgiveness, like the work of this servant, is a thankless task but it is simply our duty. It is not something for the spiritual elite, nor is it something for which you expect a medal. If you are a Christian, forgiveness is required of you."[13]

The Holy Spirit

The indwelling Spirit is needed to guide and direct leaders in the path of forgiveness. The Holy Spirit counsels and strengthens leaders in their journey and in their personal relationships with others (John 14:26). He aids them in their weaknesses, empowering them with grace to forgive rather than allowing bitterness to take root (Rom 8:26). Leaders must keep in step with the Spirit and not give way to envy, conceit, or jealousy (Gal 5:25).

Forgiveness does not diminish the gravity of the injury. Christian leaders forgive not because the injury was small but because they have been forgiven (Matt 18:23–35). Forgiveness involves looking straight into the injustice of the injury, admitting the evil that was done, accepting the darkness of the sin committed, and simultaneously choosing to let the wrong done not cause a separation between the offended and the one who committed the offence. Similarly, the Holy Spirit does not minimize sin. On the contrary, the Holy Spirit convicts the world of guilt, sin, and judgment (John 16:8). Like the Son, the Spirit first condemns the sin and then strengthens leaders with his power to accomplish the hard work of forgiveness in their own lives (Eph 3:16). Volf affirms this idea: "To forgive is to name and condemn the misdeed. The same is true of God. God doesn't just condemn and then forgive. God also condemns in the very act of forgiving."[14]

The Holy Spirit is the means by which God strengthens leaders to receive Christ's forgiveness and to forgive others. Leaders must first admit their own shortcomings and receive God's forgiveness in order to create a culture of forgiveness that will nurture and grow others into the character of Christ. Receiving God's forgiveness and forgiving oneself is essential, because everyone is human and at times will fail. Wright points out, "Organizations must create a context of forgiveness if they expect to have quality leadership. And leaders must embrace their own vulnerability and offer

---

12. Keyes, *Beyond Identity*, 148.
13. Ibid., 149.
14. Volf, *Free of Charge*, 166.

forgiveness to followers if they want to contribute to that context of forgiveness and nurture the leadership abilities of their people."[15] It is through the Holy Spirit's power that leaders can do all things, including forgiving oneself and forgiving others (Eph 1:19; Phil 4:13).

Forgiveness is necessary for leadership. Wright argues, "Forgiveness offers people the chance to take risks, to learn and to grow in their own leadership. Leaders need forgiveness given their own vulnerability and it is something they must offer others, even though others' failures increase the leaders' vulnerability."[16] Through the indwelling presence of the Holy Spirit, Christian leaders are strengthened by grace to know and receive God's forgiveness and love. Without the gift of the Holy Spirit, leaders would be unable to imitate the forgiving love of the Father (Eph 5:1). Being filled with the Holy Spirit, therefore, is essential for leaders to experience God's forgiveness and to pass on this forgiveness to others (Col 1:11–14).

Two-way communication, conflict resolution, and forgiveness are three capacities that must be developed in emerging leaders for them to be able to orchestrate change in their context. The Trinity dances these steps effortlessly, because they are intrinsic to the very nature of the *perichoresis*. Desiring to be in relationship, the Trinity enjoys two-way dialog between partners and friends. Understanding the inevitability of conflict, the God of light is ready to battle the forces of darkness to protect his children and vindicate his servants. Having experienced the pain of suffering, God demonstrates how to acknowledge wrongdoing yet, at the same time, extend a gift of relationship to wrongdoers. He invites all who follow in his dance to learn this particular step well. Understanding these three fundamental skills and developing an ease with them form the essence of the Trinity's third movement of orchestration. However, learning the movements and practicing the steps are not the point of the dance. The performance is necessary in order to truly participate in the leadership dance. This is the final movement, which is described in the next chapter.

---

15. Wright, *Relational Leadership*, 203.
16. Ibid.

8

Movement IV: Performance

Demonstration, choreography, and orchestration prepare the way for performance. Without wholeness, balance, and trust, leaders cannot lead by example. Without vision, values, and strategy, the troop members will not be coordinated well enough to dance together but will strike movement in opposite directions. Without communication, conflict resolution skills, and forgiveness, dancers soon become deaf to the Lord of the Dance. Finally, without teamwork, care, and empowerment—the steps of performance—everything is just a rehearsal and never a real accomplishment. To understand these steps, leaders must follow the model of the Trinity in perichoretic unity.

DEVELOPING TEAMWORK

Teamwork involves people developing community together and working cooperatively towards a common goal. Many organizations cluster individuals together into purported teams in an attempt to motivate them to work cooperatively. However, in reality, these clusters are nothing more than working groups. Herrington, Bonem, and Furr have identified that teams and working groups differ in two key areas: shared goals and accountability.[1] In a working group, each individual member is responsible only for personal performance. In a team, the common goal only can be achieved through the mutual, cooperative efforts of all members. As for accountability, they write, "In a working group, each individual is responsible

---

1. Herrington et al., *Leading Congregational Change*, 131.

to a supervisor. In a team, each individual is responsible to the rest of the team. It is much more challenging to be accountable to a team. It requires a level of risk that many individuals are simply not willing to accept."[2]

The ability to develop teams is essential to leadership. Organizations that fail to develop high-performance teams will not be able to reach significant goals. Patrick Lencioni observes, "Teamwork remains the ultimate competitive advantage, both because it is so powerful and so rare."[3] Christian leaders, therefore, must become adept in developing teams in order to participate in God's transformative movements. John Maxwell echoes these sentiments: "It takes teamwork to make the dream work."[4]

The Trinity: A Model of Teamwork

Since God is one, the members of the Trinity act as one, possessing the same plan, and pursue the same outcomes. The Trinity is not a working group in which one is responsible for creation, the other for redemption, and the third for sanctification. Rather, God's purpose in creation, redemption, and sanctification requires the mutual cooperative efforts of all three members, even if one specific member plays a central role in each one of the three acts. The fellowship and love that the Father, Son, and Holy Spirit demonstrate toward one another reveal that the members of the Trinity do not just cooperate with one another to complete a task but genuinely enjoy working together and striving towards the same goal.

Each member of the triune God is responsible and accountable to all the other members of the team; they each mutually submit to one another. Some have argued that the Father has preeminence in the Trinity and the Son is eternally subordinate to him.[5] Bilezikian, however, eschews any subordinationism in the Godhead, referring to scholars who try to present Christ as somehow subordinate to the Father as committing "hermeneutical bungee-jumping" maneuvers.[6] Rather than the Son and the Spirit reporting back to the Father the outcomes of their actions, there is mutual accountability and trust between all members of the Trinity.

---

2. Ibid.
3. Lencioni, *Five Dysfunctions of a Team*, vii.
4. Maxwell, *17 Indisputable Laws of Teamwork*, xiv.
5. Giles, *Trinity and Subordinationism*, 60–85.
6. Bilezikian, *Community 101*, 187–202.

Part 2: A Theology of the Trinitarian Leadership Dance

The concept of God in three persons in constant movement in a circle, as suggested by *perichoresis*, is significantly different from the more common Western symbol of the Trinity as an equilateral triangle. This is shown in figure 3 below. The three equal sides represent the equality of the three persons of the Trinity.

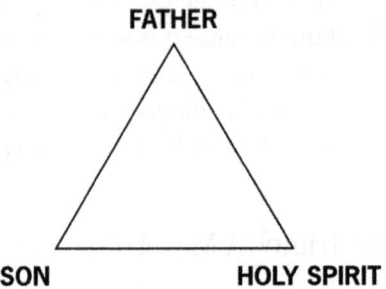

Figure 3. The Traditional Symbol for the Trinity

Over time, the corners of the triangle became erroneously linked to the three members of the Trinity, with the Father on top. This depiction reinforced a hierarchical view of God and contributed to a common notion of the subordination of the Son. What is needed is for the church to return to a "round table leadership," which reflects the circular fellowship of God.[7] The diagram in figure 4, as suggested by Guthrie, better depicts the Trinity as three divine persons dancing joyfully together, hand in hand, in a circle.[8] Equality occurs in stressing the metaphor of a circular dance, which allows each member to take a turn in leading the dance.

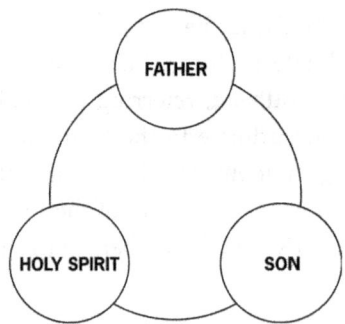

Figure 4. A Symmetrical Model of the Trinity

---

7. Russel, *Church in the Round*, 46–47, 63–67.
8. Guthrie, *Christian Doctrine*, 92.

Movement IV: Performance

Transformative teams not only are committed to a common purpose but also to the creation of a supportive community: a house of love. Figure 5 shows Andrei Rublev's famous icon of the Holy Trinity, which has the three persons of God seated around a table. Referring to this icon, Nouwen says, "I have never seen the house of love more beautifully expressed than in the icon of the Holy Trinity."[9] Similarly, ministry teams must reflect God's house of love in their attitudes and the way in which they relate to one another.

Figure 5. Andrei Rublev's Holy Trinity

This image of God in perichoretic community presents an ideal paradigm for building caring, trusting, and committed teams that are able to engage in unfiltered and passionate debate of ideas without the fear of conflict. It embodies Lencioni's five attributes of highly effective teams: trust, respect for others' views, commitment, accountability, and attention to results.[10] Moreover, the imagery of a circular dance of love conveys not only equality but also mutuality, deference, sharing, caring, harmony, inter-

9. Nouwen, *Behold the Beauty of the Lord*, 20.
10. Lencioni, *Five Dysfunctions of a Team*, 188–189.

connectedness, trusting, and collaborative activities.[11] Such vivid imagery portrays how healthy groups ought to interact with one another.

Teams must aspire to work towards God's model of community and commitment to a common purpose. The perichoretic dance of love reflects a sense of community, joy, freedom, song, intimacy, harmony, equality, unity yet distinction, and love. Similarly, ministry teams that spend time building relationships with one another create a fertile soil of trust from which spontaneity, laughter, joy, mutuality, and freedom spring. Competition is alien to such relationships, whereas genuine good will and collaboration flourish. While some might be suspicious of building such close relationships, especially amongst paid staff or lay leadership teams, in my opinion this type of teamwork reflects the heart of the Trinitarian Dance. Even though a ministry team never may reflect fully the beauty and joy of the teamwork found in the perichoretic Trinity, it is still a worthy model to emulate. Cladis concurs:

> Our leadership role must begin with an image to strive for. On the one hand is it both idyllic and absurd to think that our work groups and ministry teams could be like the Father, Son, and Spirit in perichoretic unity. . . . On the other hand, if we do *not* move toward an image, a goal, or spiritually meaningful and effective team ministry, our failure will surely result in relational breakdown, the result of human sin.[12]

EXHIBITING GENUINE CARE

Biblical leadership is about caring for people and their needs. Care is necessary for growth. Christian leaders, especially, are given a charge to care for those entrusted to their supervision (1 Pet 5:2). Each member of the Godhead exhibits this caring attitude towards one another and for people. The triune life of caring and love spills over in creative love and caring towards others.

---

11. Cladis, *Leading the Team-Based Church*, 33–155.
12. Ibid., 9.

Movement IV: Performance

The Trinity: A Model of Caring

One of God's attributes is compassion (Ps 145:9). The perichoretic unity of the triune God suggests a flow of affection, care, and concern one for the other. There is no jealousy, envy, or resentment towards the other members of the team; rather, there is support, encouragement, and congruity. The Son does not interfere with what the Spirit does, the Father is not fearful of the Son's actions, and the Spirit would not think to compete with the Father for glory or attention. Instead, they demonstrate care for one another by guarding, protecting, and trusting one another. Each seeks to give glory, honor, and praise to the other in the beautiful dance of love and life.

As well, each member of the Trinity expresses care and compassion for people. One of God's names is *Jehovah-Ra'ah*, "The Lord Is My Shepherd," as in Psalm 23:1.[13] The imagery of a shepherd connotes love and concern for the sheep. In fact, when leaders make the Lord their shepherd, God provides all the resources that they need (Ps 23:1). Instead of frantic busyness, God brings the CEO to places of rest and repose (Ps 23:2). He guides emerging leaders in the right direction and does not fail those who have walked with him for a lifetime (Ps 23:3). Even in difficult situations, God is present to comfort, discipline, and strengthen leaders in their weaknesses (Ps 23:4). He fills leaders to overflowing with blessings, even in the face of many who oppose or resist the vision (Ps 23:5). In the end, God's beauty and love chase those who put their hope and trust in him (Ps 23:6).

Similarly, Jesus cares intensely for his people. He refers to himself as the Watchman, the Gate, and the Good Shepherd (John 10:1–18). He knows each sheep by name and leads them to lush pastures (John 10:3). He lays down his life for his sheep (John 10:12), knows what is best for them (John 10:14), and cares for those who are not yet part of his sheepfold (John 10:16). His tender, loving care is comparable to a mother hen who longs to gather up chicks under her wings (Luke 13:34). After rising from the dead, he entrusts Peter with the responsibility of caring for his sheep (John 21:15–19).

The Holy Spirit also exhibits God's care and compassion, as his name is Comforter or Counselor (John 14:25; 16:7). The God of all comfort consoles individuals through the work of the Holy Spirit (2 Cor 1:3–4). Scripture invites all to cast their cares on the Lord because he sustains and cares for them (Ps 55:22: 1 Pet 5:7). The Holy Spirit intercedes for leaders

---

13. BDB, s.v. "ra'ah."

with groans and sighs too deep for words (Rom 8:26). The Holy Spirit is the means whereby God's compassion and love are experienced in a leader's life.

EMPOWERING OTHERS

Empowerment means to give power or authority to another. It is the complete opposite of grabbing power, which unfortunately is seen too often in the church, the one institution that was intended to be the antithesis of power and political games (Matt 20:25–28). Biblical leadership is not about power and control but about serving others with the gifts and talents that one has to enable others to become all that God has destined for them. In between defining reality and saying thank you, Max De Pree insists, "The leader must become a servant and a debtor."[14] Empowerment means getting down on one's hands and knees so that others can stand on one's shoulders. This is what God did, in the person of Jesus, "who did not cling to his divine power but emptied himself and became as we are"[15] (cf. Phil 2:6–8).

Responsibility comes with power and authority. Power and responsibility need to go together. Therefore, it is important to give both responsibility and authority when entrusting another with a task. L. Ford often reminds younger leaders of the Indian proverb, "Nothing grows under the Banyan tree."[16] Since banyan trees are so huge and their foliage is so thick, they do not let light through. Consequently, little seedlings are unable to grow underneath their shade. Similarly, powerful leaders are so competent and confident that they do not create space for younger leaders to experiment, learn through failure, and grow. Unless senior leaders release both responsibility and authority to their juniors—including the freedom to make mistakes and learn from them—junior leaders never will grow into their God-desired potential. Those entrusted with leadership must see their roles as not just getting tasks accomplished but, more importantly, as empowering those entrusted into their care with competence and confidence to fulfill their unique mission.

At the empowerment stage, leaders must address issues of power. Power has the ability to destroy or create. It can be used for good or for evil, to open doors or to close them, to lift up or to put down. Richard J. Foster

---

14. De Pree, *Leadership Is an art*, 9.
15. Nouwen, *In the Name of Jesus*, 58.
16. Hahn and Osterhaus, *Mentoring Tree*, 19.

describes destructive power as follows: "The power that destroys demands ascendancy; it demands total control; it destroys relationship; it destroys trust; it destroys dialog; it destroys integrity."[17] Unfortunately, destructive power produces leaders who encumber rather than enable.

The opposite of the destructive power of the world is the life-giving force of the Trinity to create, to relate, and to love. Creative power restores relationships and sets people free.[18] It produces love, humility, self-limitation, joy, vulnerability, submission, and freedom.[19] Creative influence is the result of participating in the divine dance of love and empowerment. L. Ford elaborates: "To see power as it was 'in Christ,' and to be able to use power righteously when we are 'in Christ,' acknowledges its creative or destructive potential and also admits the possibility that power itself can be redeemed from evil to good."[20]

In Christian leadership, destructive power constantly must be abandoned in favor of love.[21] Nouwen contends that the most important quality of Christian leadership in the future is not a leadership of power and control but of powerlessness and humility.[22] This means that emerging leaders must embrace their brokenness and vulnerabilities. Only when leaders lead from Christ's power and strength will they effectively display the kingdom of light. L. Ford elucidates, "Next to truth, the power question is the most important issue for the leader."[23] Leaders must be fully convinced that effectiveness comes through enabling others to reach their potential—both personal and corporate— rather than controlling, domineering, or following proper procedures.[24]

The Trinity: A Model of Empowerment

The image of God as a communion of three persons in a divine circle dance suggests mutuality and reciprocity. Such a picture of mutuality "shatters

---

17. Foster, *Challenge of the Disciplined Life*, 175.
18. Ibid., 196 and 198.
19. Ibid., 201–6.
20. L. Ford, *Transforming Leadership*, 143.
21. Nouwen, *In the Name of Jesus*, 63.
22. Ibid.
23. Ford, *Transforming Leadership*, 140.
24. De Pree, *Leadership Is an Art*, 16.

Part 2: A Theology of the Trinitarian Leadership Dance

all human images of [power and] domination."[25] Instead, the *kenosis* (or self-emptying)[26] of the Son portrays servanthood more than domination. Fiddes asserts that the language of the Trinity is more about interdependence and participation than power and control.[27] *Perichoresis* connotes diversity, difference, and mutuality rather than supremacy as a source of power. Fiddes shows how the image of the triune God critiques all human power structures and invites humans instead to become fully engaged in God's dance of empowerment.[28]

Christian leaders graciously are invited to participate in this divine dance of love and empowerment and, consequently, must guard themselves against any thoughts of supremacy. Nouwen warns, "Ever since the snake said, 'The day you eat of this tree your eyes will be open and you will be like gods, knowing good from evil,' we have been tempted to replace love with power."[29] Instead, leaders must have a humble attitude of a servant and a grateful spirit towards those who provide opportunities for them to minister. Moreover, leaders must raise a "prophetic voice of protest" against all forms of domination and absolute power and "release people from the wish to be dominated by what seems to promise protection and security."[30]

In order to empower others, leaders must give sacrificially and voluntarily of themselves. Sacrificial, self-giving love is what characterizes the fellowship of the Father, Son, and Holy Spirit as each member of the Godhead seeks to empower and exalt the others. This is "the very heart of the Trinity,"[31] or the "Trinity's signature,"[32] which reveals the very inner life of God. "Before the world was," says Moltmann, "the sacrifice was already in God. No Trinity is conceivable without the Lamb, without the sacrifice of love, without the crucified Son."[33] Paradoxically, each of the triune persons freely lays himself down for the sake of the other two and, in the very act of losing his life, finds it in eternal joyous communion with others. Geoffrey Wainwright observes, "The divine Persons empty themselves into each and

25. Fiddes, *Participating in God*, 69.
26. BDAG, s.v. "kenoó."
27. Fiddes, *Participating in God*, 3–108.
28. Ibid.
29. Nouwen, *In the Name of Jesus*, 60.
30. Ibid., 69–70.
31. Ibid., 78.
32. Leupp, *Knowing the Name of God*, 28.
33. Moltmann, *Trinity and the Kingdom*, 83.

Movement IV: Performance

receive each other's fullness."[34] By participating in this divine dance of self-sacrifice and self-giving love, leaders win followers' hearts through humble service and discover that the only authority lies in being trusted.[35]

God, the Almighty

God in the Old Testament is referred to as *'Ēl 'Elyōn*, "The Most High God," "The Almighty."[36] He is the supreme ruler, who controls nations and history. All of creation is sustained by his power (Ps 103) and all events are in his hands (Eccl 9:1). The name "The Almighty" suggests that all power and might belong to him who sits on the throne and rules over heaven and earth (Rev 11:17). This sovereign God of power and might is the one who provides everything for humanity and empowers them with the ability to choose (Gen 2:15–16).

The Almighty God, however, also is revealed as a loving Father in the Scriptures (Deut 32:6; Jer 3:4,19; Isa 64:8; Matt 6:9). He longs to be in relationship with his children in order to lift them up and empower them to be all that he created them to be. He is a father who delights to be addressed by the intimate term *Abba* (Matt 6:9; Rom 8:15; Gal 4:6), who is merciful (Luke 6:36), who waits out anxiously on the road for the return of a prodigal son (Luke 15), and who searches for his children like a woman searching for lost coins (Luke 15). In contrast to a Platonic understanding of God as the Father and Maker of the universe who stands in complete transcendence and remoteness to the finite created world, this Father is the Father of the Son whose love is so intense and overflowing that he desires other sons and daughters to share in their relationship. Fiddes clarifies, "The divine longing is for the movements of the dance between Father and Son to be opened up to include a myriad of other partners."[37] This image of a Father who cares and even suffers for his children to allow them entrance into an intimate dance of love rejects all other images of dominance, power, or control.

---

34. Wainright, *Doxology*, 23.
35. Fiddes, *Participation in God*, 100.
36. BDB, s.v. "elyōwn."
37. Fiddes, *Participation in God*, 95.

Part 2: A Theology of the Trinitarian Leadership Dance

Jesus Christ, the Son

Jesus Christ had ultimate power and authority as the second person of the Godhead, yet he chose to empty himself of that power and become incarnate as a human being (Phil 2:4–6). L. Ford observes, "No one ever had at their disposal greater powers than Jesus . . . yet, he held these powers not with a closed fist, but with an open hand, as something received and to be given."[38] When tempted to use his power for personal ends, to grasp for power, or to use his supernatural power to command God's attention, Jesus refused (Luke 4:3–12). He knew what kind of power and authority he had; he knew he possessed unusual powers and that the Father had entrusted everything to him; still, he modeled servanthood to his disciples by washing their feet (John 13:1–17). Jesus explained to Pilate that since his kingdom was not of this world, his servants did not fight to prevent his arrest (John 18:36). In fact, Pilate would have had no power over him had it not been granted from above (John 19:11). Even now, Jesus holds all power and authority in heaven and earth, yet he stoops down to serve humankind with his self-sacrificial love (Matt 28:18; Rom 5:8).

Jesus did not hoard power but freely enabled his disciples to do whatever he was doing. He gave them power and authority to cast out demons and heal the sick when he sent them out to preach the kingdom of God (Luke 9:1). He taught them through on-the-job training. When they were unable to perform a ministry task, Jesus used these teachable moments to impress upon them the power of prayer (Mark 9:14–28). Even today, believers have been granted the fullness of Christ, including his power and authority (Col 2:10).

When Jesus' disciples argued about who was the greatest, Jesus placed a little child in their midst in order to show them that greatness involves humbling oneself like a child and serving others (Matt 18:1–4; Mark 9:33–37; Luke 9:46–48). In doing so, "he was pointing to the ability of children to work and play without the need for supremacy."[39] He rebuked them when they argued about greatness, insisting that self-sacrifice and service was the path to greatness (Matt 20:20–28; Mark 10:35–45; Luke 22:24–30). He turned their thinking about power upside down when he contrasted the way the rulers of the Gentiles lead with the way that servants in the kingdom should lead. He harshly condemned "power over" someone and

---

38. L. Ford, *Transforming Leadership*, 144.
39. Foster, *Challenge of the Disciplined Life*, 177.

instead advocated for his disciples to exercise "power under," the power that washes people's feet and uplifts others. He demonstrated that influence in others' lives is only obtained when one humbly serves. He repeatedly impressed upon their hearts and lives that "in the kingdom of God the issue of greatness is an issue that is beside the point."[40]

The Holy Spirit

The Holy Spirit empowers ordinary believers to be able to live the life of Christ, because he dwells inside them. Paul likens the working of the Holy Spirit as God's "incomparably great power" that raised Christ from the dead (Eph 1:18,19). In other words, the Holy Spirit's explosive power is a reality that leaders can experience and tap into so that they can do everything to which God calls them (Phil 4:13). God does not call leaders without first anointing and empowering them with the Holy Spirit to fulfill the assignment entrusted to them (Judg 2:18).

Not only does the Holy Spirit empower believers with his presence, he gives each believer spiritual gifts (1 Cor 12:4-6). In fact, each person of the divine Trinity works in distributing spiritual gifts to the church. In 1 Corinthians 12:4-6, there are three parallel causes: "Different kinds of gifts but the same Spirit . . . different kinds of service but the same Lord . . . different kinds of workings but the same God." There are "clear trinitarian implications," remarks Gordon D. Fee, "in this set of sentences, the earliest of such texts in the New Testament," for they are the "stuff from which later theological constructs are correctly derived."[41] It is important that leaders know their spiritual gifts so that they minister from their strengths. Although discovering and developing one's spiritual gifts is the responsibility of each believer, God also has given apostles, pastors, evangelists, teachers, and prophets to assist the Body of Christ in this quest (Eph 4:11-12).

The Holy Spirit empowers by filling believers with his presence, bestowing spiritual gifts, and also by giving leaders to the church so that they will equip and develop people (Eph 4:11-13). This is the sacred trust that God has given every Christian leader: "to prepare God's people for works of service, so that the body of Christ may be built up" (Eph 4:12). When Christian leaders hang on to controlling hierarchical mental constructs of leadership rather than shifting to empowering, supportive paradigms

---

40. Ibid.

41. Fee, *First Epistle to the Corinthians*, 588.

of ministry, they despise God's trust and trample on his people. Rather, Christian leaders must enter into Christ's ministry of empowerment, take up the basin and the towel, and sacrificially serve God's people so that they can become all that God desires them to be.

Teamwork, care, and empowerment are the final steps in the Trinitarian Dance. Creating loving and cooperative teams that are responsive to the needs of an organization and mutually accountable for the shared outcomes are an essential catalyst for transformation. Leaders must know how to create guiding coalitions to facilitate lasting change. Loving care and concern for one another develops community and communicates belonging to many who feel isolated and alone. Finally, empowerment is the *sine qua non* of Christian leadership. Emerging leaders must learn and practice these essential steps not only to achieve results but, more importantly, to discover real joy and satisfaction in the dance of leadership.

Part 3

Church-Based Strategies for the Trinitarian Leadership Dance

PART 3

9

The Trinitarian Dance of Leader Development in the Local Church

Identifying and developing leaders is a primary function of leadership.[1] Since there is a dearth of leaders in the Canadian church, we must do everything possible to identify, train, and equip leaders for its future. The purpose of this section is to provide practical and realistic strategies to guide pastors and leaders in creating leadership development communities within their own local churches. As pastors familiarize themselves with the steps and movements of the Trinitarian Dance, and as they dance them creatively in their own contexts, they will discover the joy and lightness of letting God lead them in the dance.

WELCOMING THE MOVEMENTS OF THE TRIUNE GOD

One of the most frustrating experiences for those learning new skills is encountering people who think that everyone else instinctively should know how to do something for which they are uniquely gifted. Gifted people make terrible teachers. Since they are gifted, they simply expect others to pick up on their skills like they did. Similarly, if people are great leaders, it may be hard for them to develop other leaders simply because it comes naturally to them. The Trinitarian Dance, however, provides an excellent means to make the implicit explicit.

---

1. Clinton, *Making of a Leader*, 196.

Part 3: Church-Based Strategies for the Trinitarian Leadership Dance

Using the Trinitarian Dance as a framework, learning communities can be created to study and practice the movements of the Trinity's leadership dance. McNeal states, "The new methodology for developing apostolic leaders involves an intentional process called the learning community."[2] Creating safe and supportive communities where honest feedback is sought is the primary task of the pastor. In order to bring about life transformation, such learning communities must have three ingredients: transparent trust, truth of God's Word, and mutual accountability.[3] Greg Ogden convincingly argues that a triad is the ideal size to cultivate these elements, though clusters of six or ten are also effective.[4] Consequently, pastors could create small-group-sized learning communities and encourage more intimate accountability triads for genuine life change.

Developing any skill takes patience and perseverance. Welcoming the movements means learning all four Trinitarian Dance movements with others and developing an ease and familiarity with each of the twelve steps. It requires demonstrating Christlikeness in one's own character, seeing God's vision for one's own life, being purified through conflict, and humbled to serve and strengthen others. As leaders develop proficiency with the movements, they pay attention to God's activity in their own journeys and listen for how God is moving in the journeys of others as well.

This pattern and flow of transformational leadership development can be depicted in a matrix (see figure 6 below). Christian leadership development begins and ends at the center with one's identity as a beloved child of God, similar to the warm-up exercises and cooling stretches that dancers do prior to and after their performance. In the first movement of demonstration, character development and spiritual formation are key. Moving clockwise to choreography, developing leaders gain clarity about the unique vision, values, and strategy that God is casting in their lives. Continuing clockwise through the movements of orchestration and performance, leaders work out the implications of the dance for their own lives and ministries. As emerging leaders progress through all four movements, they gain valuable insights into their character and God's vision for their lives. By practicing these steps in real life, they gain familiarity with the twelve steps in the Trinity's leadership dance. Cycling through the four movements again gives emerging leaders an increased awareness and familiarity with

2. McNeal, *Revolution in Leadership*, 18.
3. Ogden, *Transforming Discipleship*, 172.
4. Ibid.

these skills. Each time through these four movements takes leaders to greater and greater depths. The result is a mature, secure leader with a focused calling and the strategic expertise to fulfill it.

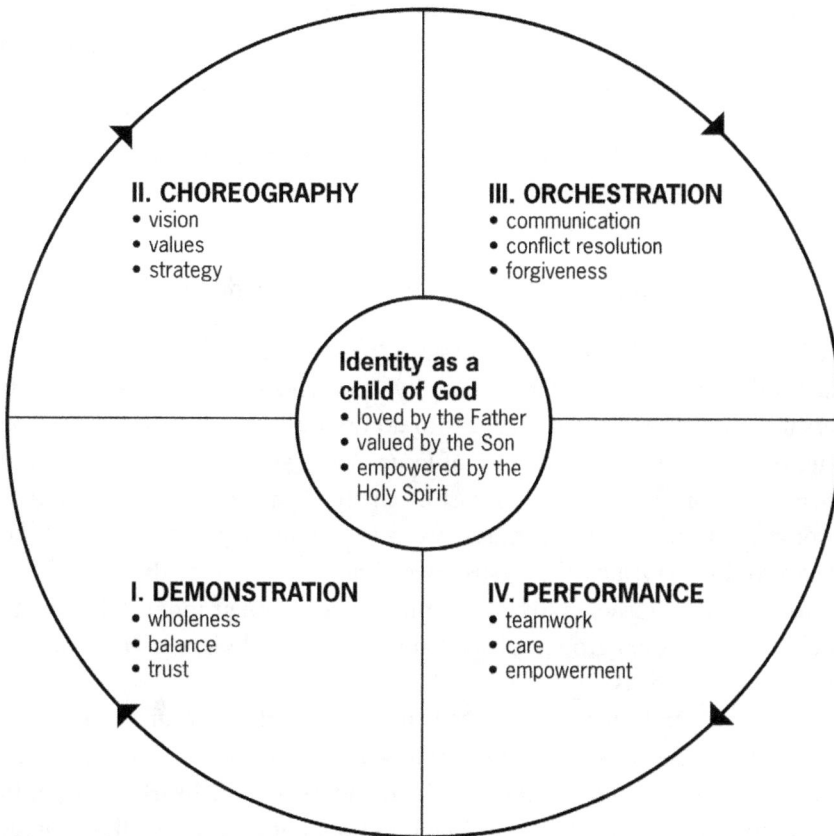

Figure 6. The Trinitarian Leadership Dance

In order to train leaders, some type of learning environment must be created. One method would be to offer twelve seminars on each of the twelve steps. These seminars could be offered as single units (i.e., twelve sessions) or over a longer period of time. For instance, focusing on one step for an entire month provides Christian education for an entire year. Another strategy would be to form a small group of emerging leaders and meet with them for a set period of time. An alternative means is to take existing leaders and arrange training sessions around their schedules, perhaps once a month for a period of a year. Another idea is to schedule three retreats,

Part 3: Church-Based Strategies for the Trinitarian Leadership Dance

each focusing on one member of the Trinity and on four of the steps. One might even consider offering three courses—one on the Father, one on the Son, and one on the Holy Spirit—each focusing on the twelve steps through the lens of one member of the Trinity. The possibilities are endless. The key is to structure training so that there is a committed learning community, a learning process over time, spiraled learning to reinforce steps previously introduced, and accountability to ensure genuine life change. Each leader must dance with the Trinity, following the Holy Spirit's lead, to design training that is suitable within one's own context.

Demonstration: The Bedrock of Leadership

It is imperative that leaders not skip demonstration. This first phase is about developing character or integrity; it establishes the bedrock of leadership. It is not enough for leaders to do the right thing; they must be the right people, reflecting the heart of Jesus. Asking others to change without being willing to risk the high cost of change is at best ineffective and at worse hypocritical. Leaders must choose to become apprenticed to Jesus, to learn to do everything that Jesus does.[5] The main goal for this movement is for developing leaders to become more aware of their inner states and to develop intentional growth plans that bring more wholeness, balance, and trust into their lives.

Demonstration starts with self-discovery. McNeal confirms this, saying, "The single most vital piece of information a leader needs is an understanding of who he or she is."[6] Being aware of one's heart is central in gauging emotional intelligence.[7] The Emotional/Spiritual Health Inventory is one helpful assessment in determining emotional maturity in developing leaders.[8] The trust assessment of Stephen M. R. Covey and Rebecca R. Merrill help developing leaders determine their strengths and weaknesses in four areas: integrity, intent, capabilities, and results.[9] There are

---

5. Willard with Matthews, "Spirituality and Ministry."
6. McNeal, *Revolution in Leadership*, 82.
7. Goleman, *Emotional Intelligence*, 43.
8. Scazzero, *Emotionally Healthy Church*, 60–66.
9. Covey with Merrill, *Speed of Trust*, 50–53.

many other assessment tools that rate spiritual well-being,[10] Christian life,[11] and anxiety.[12] Others include assertiveness,[13] stress,[14] self-differentiation,[15] burnout,[16] and intimacy,[17] along with online assessments for subjects like emotional intelligence, anger, depression, mental health, leadership style, learning style, and the like.[18] A battery of assessments and personality inventories at the beginning of the training process gives emerging leaders a deeper self-understanding and helps them determine which areas require attention.

Despite all these assessments, however, many leaders do not take enough time to reflect on their inner reality. Pue outlines three reasons why leaders lack self-awareness: lack of feedback, insecurity, and busyness.[19] Self-reflection and honest, constructive feedback are critical to spiritual formation in Christlikeness. Therefore, these two elements must be included in any training program. Pue refers to this initial phase in leadership development as the "freeing up" phase where younger leaders examine their core needs and where they are turning to have them met.[20] Learning to satisfy these needs by legitimate means is one of the objectives of the first movement.

Demonstration begins with wholeness and inner peace. When leaders lead from a sense of wholeness rather than from frenetic activity, fewer people are hurt and God's plans and purposes are realized in unimaginable ways. When leaders rest secure in their identity as God's children and not in the power or their position, they are free to follow the leading of the

---

10. Lawson and Carter, "Personal Ministry Integration: Spiritual Well-Being, Ellison, 1983."

11. Lawson and Carter, "Personal Ministry Integration: Christian Life Assessment Scales"; see also Frazee, *Christian Life Profile*.

12. Hart, "Self-Rating Anxiety Scale."

13. Hart, "The Assertiveness Inventory."

14. Hart, "Stress Test."

15. Hart, "Checklist for Self-Differentiation."

16. Hart, "Burnout Checklist."

17. Hart, "Intimacy Scale for Couple Work."

18. Many online assessments can be found at Queendom: The Land of Tests (www.queendom.com). See also Mehrabian, "Personality & Communication"; and Chapman, "Management Skill Set Assessment."

19. Pue, *Mentoring Leaders*, 32–38.

20. Ibid., 21.

Part 3: Church-Based Strategies for the Trinitarian Leadership Dance

Holy Spirit rather than be manipulated by power brokers or the agendas of others.

God desires to bring *shalom* to every aspect of a leader's life. Peace is a sign of spiritual maturity. As one matures in one's personal spiritual walk, anxiety and drivenness decrease while inner peace increases.[21] The church fathers and mystics of the past affirm that growing into a life of peace, exhibited by a lifestyle of love, is the ultimate goal and hallmark of spiritual maturity. Janet O. Hagberg and Robert A. Guelich describe living "the life of love," characterized by a "quiet, unassuming way," as the sixth and final stage in "the critical journey."[22] Knowing one's identity as God's child (the warm-up in the trinitarian leadership dance) reminds leaders that they are loved, valued, and capable. Leading learning communities in spiritual exercises that focus on these three aspects of the Trinity can be a very powerful method of spiritual discovery for young leaders.[23] In addition, leaders who pursue God's *shalom* deep in their inner being are serious about depending on the Father for their strength and seek to eliminate all striving or working in the flesh. One simple question can be asked of developing leaders: "On a continuum between one and ten, how peaceful would you describe your life?"[24] Their answer reveals the degree of *shalom* that they are experiencing. Having intercessors pray over those with anxious spirits and providing opportunities for those with wounded spirits to experience God's inner healing is an invaluable gift to emerging leaders.

In order to live in better balance, the second aspect of demonstration, leaders must practice Willard's golden triangle. Willard describes the process of "putting on the Lord Jesus Christ" (Eph 4:22–24) as the "golden triangle" of transformation. It is golden because the results are as precious as pure gold to the disciple, and, since each aspect is essential to the whole

---

21. Ibid., 40.

22. Hagberg and Guelich, *Critical Journey*, 151–60.

23. One spiritual exercise that can be used is the following: (1) lead the group in a time of silence; (2) read Jeremiah 31:3, then invite them to silently reflect on, "Father, you love me;" (3) after a minute, read 1 Peter 5:7 and then ask participants to silently meditate on, "Jesus, you care for me;" (4) after another minute, read John 15:16a and encourage them to pray, "Holy Spirit, you're going to use me today;" (5) debrief after one more minute of silence by asking them to share their impressions and feelings; and, (6) encourage them to meditate on these three statements during the upcoming week. Another exercise could make use of the statements from "Who I Am in Christ," in Anderson and Mylander, *Setting your Church Free*, 359.

24. Pue, *Mentoring Leaders*, 40.

process, there are three sides to the triangle.[25] The first side of the triangle is faithful acceptance of everyday problems. The second side is interaction with God's Holy Spirit in and around us. The third side is the spiritual disciplines, namely solitude, silence, study, secrecy, fasting, or worship.[26] The spiritual disciplines expand one's ability to live in harmony with the Holy King's rule and reign in one's life. Discussing spiritual disciplines with developing leaders and introducing them to some of the essential disciplines will help them grow in spiritual formation. The learning objective of this step is for emerging leaders to become aware of the spiritual disciplines, to reflect on the benefits of their use, and to plan how to incorporate them into their spiritual journeys.

Leaders also must be balanced in their relationship with the Father, Son, and Holy Spirit. Schwarz has developed a model called the "Trinitarian Compass" and a survey called the "Color Profile" as tools to determine the strength of one's relationship to each member of the Trinity. While criticized as having a completely "economic" approach,[27] because he assigns different functions to different members of the Trinity, Schwarz's intention is to encourage believers to seek "a radical sense of balance" in their relationship with Father, Son, and Holy Spirit: "to be as committed as possible in all three areas: radically Christ-centered . . . radically ministering in the power of the Holy Spirit . . . and radically focused on God's creation."[28] These instruments can be used by both churches and individuals to strengthen their relationship with God by focusing on the person of the Trinity with whom they are least connected. By using them, leaders can determine imbalance, alert believers to the danger connected with such imbalance, and create an atmosphere of unity through an understanding of the different color zones.

To be effective and productive, leaders must be able to trust and be trusted. De Pree observes, "When trust permeates a group, great things are possible, not the least of which is a true opportunity to reach our potential."[29] Building trust and being trustworthy are how leaders earn the confidence of others. Trusting the Trinity more expands one's own trustworthiness. Just as the Father, Son, and Holy Spirit are genuine, faithful, and true, pastors

---

25. Willard, *Great Omission*, 26–30.

26. For a list of spiritual disciplines see Willard, *Spirit of the Disciplines*, 158; and Foster, *Celebration of Discipline*, v.

27. Edgar, *Message of the Trinity*, 27.

28. Schwarz, *Color Your World with Natural Church Development*, 54.

29. De Pree, *Leading Without Power*, 123.

must be authentic, dependable, and truth-tellers. A ruthless commitment to the truth and to reality is one of the capacities needed if leaders are to be healthy and growing.

The Speed of Trust explains why personal credibility is the foundation of all trust and how to create it by examining four cores: integrity, intent, capabilities, and results. He also lists thirteen behaviors which increase relational trust. As emerging leaders discuss these core areas, behaviors, and principles of increasing credibility in learning communities, they will grasp why those who are faithful in little things can be entrusted with greater responsibilities (Matt 25:21).[30] One objective for this step is for emerging leaders to become sensitive to the issues of trust and to seek to build trust with their coworkers in ministry.

The main purpose of demonstration is not only to model Christlikeness but also to encourage developing leaders to create an intentional growth plan that will bring greater wholeness, balance, and trust in their own lives. It might take the form of a personal prescription for health,[31] or one might utilize a template provided by some denominations.[32] Alternatively, one might invite emerging leaders to create their own categories, state their objectives for each category, how they will accomplish these objectives, and how they will assess whether or not they have met their objectives.[33] These growth plans must be written down, for plans that are not written down are forgotten easily. Ensuring that emerging leaders have a support base to keep them accountable is vital to guaranteeing the long-term success of the growth plan.

Choreography: The Inspiration of Leadership

The choreography of a musical involves hearing the music, matching the right character with the right actor, and arranging the steps of the dance scenes. Similarly, leaders must hear God's music, match biblical values with organizational intent, and map out a realistic plan of implementation. Vision, values, and strategy are the steps of the second movement of the Trinity's dance. Dialoguing about these themes with developing leaders is

---

30. Covey with Merrill, *Speed of Trust*, 41–230. Other resources for discussing trust include Quinn, *Deep Change*, and Kouzes and Posner, *Credibility*.

31. Hart, "Minister's Personal Growth."

32. DeGraaf, "Personal Growth Plan Handbook."

33. Lawson and Carter, "Personal Ministry Integration."

important in aiding them in acquiring the capacities to turn vision into reality. The main learning objective for this movement is to help emerging leaders to sharpen their vision, discover their values, and understand the dynamics of change. The use of case studies, simulations, experiential exercises, and project planning are some of the means to accomplish these objectives.

Hybels describes vision as the "fuel that leaders run on," "the energy that creates action," "the fire that ignites the passion of followers," "the clear call that sustains focused effort year after year," and "the most potent weapon in a leader's arsenal."[34] This is why it is so important for leaders to help other leaders sharpen their vision. L. Ford makes it a habit to ask younger leaders, "What is your vision?" If they are not sure, he asks, "If you did have one, what would it be?"[35]

Leaders receive God's vision through prayer (Amos 3:7). Then, they enter into a process of observing, reflecting, and acting.[36] They observe where God is working and where they can make a difference. They reflect on their observations in light of Scripture and other valuable readings. Then, they act in small ways on what they have observed and reflected on to grow in their leadership. It requires original, creative thinking. Hybels delineates three steps in clarifying vision: seeing the vision, feeling deeply about it so that one inspires others, and taking responsibility for it.[37]

Disciples are responsible for stewarding God's vision for their lives and bringing their decisions into alignment with God's purposes. There are certain conditions of the heart that enable disciples to hear God's voice and see his vision more clearly. Humility and love for God stand out as two essential conditions. Pue lists twelve items that often are the cause of a blurred vision that can be discussed in learning clusters.[38] Many have written good discussion questions to help sharpen vision.[39] The learning objective in this step is for emerging leaders to receive God's vision for their life and ministry.

---

34. Hybels, *Courageous Leadership*, 31 and 50.

35. Ford, "Helping Leaders Grow," 133.

36. Ford, *Transforming Leadership*, 116.

37. Hybels, *Courageous Leadership*, 36–37.

38. Conditions that blur vision are busyness, comfort, too many options, insecurity, unresolved past issues, laziness, good things keeping one from great things, pressure, another's vision, no expectation for vision, and secret sins. Pue, *Mentoring Leaders*, 106.

39. Some good discussion questions can be found in the following: Pue, *Mentoring Leaders*, 121; Barna, *Power of Vision*, 79–94; Hybels, *Courageous Leadership*, 38.

Case studies and dialog surrounding these questions will assist developing leaders to gain focus in their vision quest.[40]

Discovering the importance of values and recognizing their complexity is the next learning objective of choreography. By delineating the different types of values and discussing their importance, emerging leaders will understand their own values and the necessity of creating conscious, shared values within the ministries that they lead. Asking developing leaders to distinguish between an actual core value and a desired value that they have is one way to help them differentiate between different types of values. Conducting an audit of core values will enable them to discover their own set of values and provide them with a tool for developing values within their own context.[41] Another learning objective of this step is for developing leaders to become familiar with the Trinity's values and adopt them. Asking emerging leaders to reflect on the Trinity's core values and exposing them to the concept of *perichoresis* will help sharpen their theological reflection. Finally, discussing value clashes within their own context or in case studies will impress on them the urgency to identify shared values before such clashes occur.

To implement strategy, the third step of choreography, emerging leaders must know the change process[42] and the change disciplines.[43] The world is altering rapidly. Transformation does not happen overnight. It takes patience, perseverance, and skill to produce successful life-transformational shifts in systems and organizations. Leading people and transforming systems are complex and infinitely more difficult than one can imagine.

---

40. A good case study is Robert Kuhn, "Death of a Dream, Birth of a Vision," in Pue, *Mentoring Leaders*, 115–21.

41. Two core values audits can be found in Malphurs, *Values-Driven Leadership*, 185–87.

42. Kotter, *Leading Change*, 21, outlines an eight-stage process of creating a major change as follows: establishing a sense of urgency, creating the guiding coalition, developing a vision and strategy, communicating the change vision, empowering broad-based action, generating short-term wins, consolidating gains and producing more change, anchoring new approaches in the culture. Herrington et al., *Leading Congregational Change*, 12, have modified Kotter's model slightly to describe the change process within congregations: making personal preparation, creating urgency, establishing the vision community, discerning the vision and determining the vision path, communicating the vision, empowering change leaders, implementing the vision, and reinforcing momentum through alignment.

43. The change disciplines are creative tension, mental models, team learning, and systems thinking; in Herrington et al., *Leading Congregational Change*, 99.

The Trinitarian Dance of Leader Development in the Local Church

The demand for change and continuous learning is stressful for leaders. Herrington, Bonem, and Furr stress that spiritual vitality together with the change process and learning disciplines are essential to successful transformations.[44] They assert, "It is not enough to know that change is needed, or even to have a clear image of the church's future. The challenge is to create a realistic way to get there."[45] Case studies and role-playing are two effective means of getting younger leaders to think critically about leading change. Dreaming about changing some aspect in their own ministry and submitting a project proposal is another method to start thinking about the change process and change disciplines. The learning objective in the strategy section is for leaders to experience the change process and the change disciplines in a real-life setting. Discussing their projects and aiding the implementation of those projects are effective ways for them to experience leading change.

Orchestration: The Persistence of Leadership

Implementing God's vision through successful orchestration requires courage, compassion, and vital dependence on the Holy Spirit. The main learning objective for orchestration is for developing leaders to practice two-way communication, to become familiar with different conflict management styles, and to experience the freedom and release of forgiving from the heart. Communicating the vision is the first step in strategic planning. Conflict often is part of the process, so resolution skills and forgiveness are needed to keep leaders in the center of the Trinitarian Dance of love. Learning these capacities involves practicing communication exercises, analyzing case studies, role-playing, and praying with those who need to forgive. Honesty and vulnerability at this stage are important to model transparency and to create a safe environment where participants willingly share openly. When emerging leaders implement their projects in their own context, they will gain familiarity with two-way communication skills, conflict resolution skills, and forgiveness.

Without the ability to communicate with enthusiasm and clarity, the vision can be lost easily. As presented in chapter 7, God favors two-way communication over telling or commanding others. Effective communication encourages the exchange of thoughts, ideas, and feelings to support

---

44. Ibid., 14–15.
45. Ibid., 12.

understanding and social connection; it is a process and an ongoing activity. Vision is cast, and feedback is received and incorporated into new plans and strategies. Effective communicators adapt flexibly to each situation depending on the feedback received. By performing active listening and coaching exercises, developing leaders will have confidence to exercise two-way communication in ministry situations. Actually soliciting feedback on their project proposals also helps them to experience two-way communication.

Conflict is to be expected in leadership. Obstacles abound when leaders move forward with God's transformative vision. Perceived threats, however, can be turned into opportunities. While conflict is unpleasant, God uses it to mold leaders. McNeal states, "Spiritual leaders must welcome conflict as a heart-shaping tool of God."[46] Emerging leaders need to understand that conflict is normal and inevitable. In fact, the lack of conflict may indicate a reluctance to take risks. McNeal delineates eight strategies for dealing with conflict. He advises leaders to get over it, choose the pain, examine one's critics, look in the mirror, get good advice, be kind and honest, and forgive.[47] Discussing these strategies and discovering new strategies is an activity that learning communities can do together to become aware of how to deal with conflict in their own situations.

In addition, developing leaders must become conversant about different conflict management styles. Over time, everyone develops a personal conflict management style, which is learned by experience and can be changed. Conflict management style assessments,[48] case studies, simulations, and discussion of real-life conflict situations are tools that will assist developing leaders to become aware of their own personal style and identify others' styles. Not only understanding the various styles but also being able to change one's style to become more collaborative is one of the learning objectives of this phase.

Moreover, developing leaders need to be able to differentiate between life-giving and life-threatening conflict and to be able to discern how God is using conflict in their own journeys. Life-threatening conflict occurs when people are more concerned with their own comfort than with the achievement of God's plan. When this happens, the conflict eclipses the vision,

46. McNeal, *Work of Heart*, 156.

47. Ibid., 156–74.

48. There are many conflict management style assessments online, including Falikowski, "What's Your Conflict Management Style."

The Trinitarian Dance of Leader Development in the Local Church

whereas life-giving conflict occurs when people genuinely seek God's will in response to a sharp disagreement.[49] Often, developing leaders are caught unaware whenever resistance to change arises. A learning community can help greatly during this state to assist developing leaders in becoming aware of God's sovereign use of conflict to mold and shape their character and lives after his own heart.

The last step in orchestration is forgiveness. Forgiveness is an important aspect of conflict resolution. Most conflict involves not simply sharp disagreement but, more often than not, some kind of personal pain. Forgiveness stands at the heart of the Trinity, since the mission of the Son was to bring forgiveness to humanity and bring people back into a relationship with the Father. Similarly, leaders must choose and keep on choosing to forgive, because without forgiveness they simply are not dancing to the tune of the Trinity's dance of love. Developing leaders need to be reminded that forgiveness occurs because they have been forgiven a much greater debt by the Father (Matt 18:21–35). Biblical teaching and praying for healing are two practical ways to impress this vital truth into emerging leaders' hearts and souls.

The learning objective for this step is to experience the freedom and release of forgiving from the heart. Devotionals on biblical characters who endured great suffering and forgave, like Joseph (Gen 37–50), are helpful in reminding developing leaders of the importance of forgiveness. Honest and vulnerable sharing about one's own struggles in the area of forgiveness creates an atmosphere of transparency and brokenness. Listening to, praying for, and helping developing leaders process and release their pain enables them to forgive honestly from the heart. Those suffering from childhood wounds or deeper pain may need to be referred to a counselor to help them cut through the defensive walls of protection they may have built around themselves. Inviting the Holy Spirit to guide and direct these sessions on forgiveness can bring significant insight and awareness in this area.

Performance: The Joy of Leadership

Performance brings all the other steps of the Trinity's perichoretic dance together, for it is about sustaining the vision and pressing onwards to the goal with others. The main learning objectives in this movement is for emerging leaders to be able to identify the principles of good teamwork, to

49. Herrington et al., *Leading Congregational Change*, 8–9.

comprehend the value of creating caring cultures within their teams, and to be able to use situational leadership to empower and motivate their team members. To be able to grasp these principles, developing leaders can be invited to build a team to implement their project.

Emerging leaders must become team-oriented and reproducing.[50] Coaching emerging leaders in the development of teams is important so they will have a support base that will advance their ministry. Introducing the five dysfunctions of a team, participating in team-building exercises, and assessing their own team will offer valuable insights for emerging leaders.[51] The learning objectives for this section are to help developing leaders distinguish between working groups and teams, to assess their current team's susceptibility to the five dysfunctions, and to encourage them to build stronger relationships within their teams. Cladis argues that teams must incorporate seven attributes, which he distills from exploring the perichoretic communion of Father, Son, and Holy Spirit.[52] Three of these attributes—covenanting, collaborating, and learning—are aspects of team building crucial to this stage.

Effective leaders create an ethos of care, hospitality, and openness for one another. Since "the community of the Father, Son, and Spirit is a culture of love,"[53] leaders must learn how to create communities of love. People will not buy into the vision without first buying into the leader.[54] This makes caring so important. One aspect of great leaders is exhibiting genuine care and concern for the success of their followers. Following in the footsteps of the Good Shepherd creates the desire to become a good shepherd towards others.

Modeling a caring posture towards the members of the learning community speaks louder than mere words. Since the demands of leadership are so great, it is easy to become so busy that leaders neglect this basic attitude of caring for others. "Haste," declares Willard, "is the enemy of Christ's life flowing in and through us."[55] Therefore, disciples must "ruthlessly eliminate

---

50. McNeal, *Revolution in Leadership*, 29.

51. An assessment can be found in Lencioni, *Five Dysfunctions of a Team*, 192–94.

52. The seven attributes are: covenanting, visioning, culture creating, collaborating, trusting, empowering, and learning; in Cladis, *Leading the Team-Based Church*, 33–155. The entire book addresses these attributes in detail.

53. Ibid., 12.

54. Maxwell, *21 Irrefutable Laws of Leadership*, 143–51.

55. Willard with Matthews, "Spirituality and Ministry."

hurry from their lives" if they desire to express love and compassion like Christ.[56] Sharing personal life experiences about the tyranny of the urgent and discussing one's strengths and weaknesses in showing compassion will impress upon young leaders the importance of caring. Practicing caring within the community expresses concern for each of individual, which will motivate them to care for others.

Taking the time to listen and mentor emerging leaders communicates care. L. Ford is renowned for nurturing emerging leaders. At his "Leading from Within" retreats,[57] he intently listens to each younger leader's story and makes himself available to leaders who are sometimes less than half his age. His humility, gentleness, Christlike love, and wisdom have inspired me to emulate that kind of nurture for emerging leaders whom I am developing. His care and nurture for me without any strings attached reflect the heart of the Trinity's care for his people. The learning objective for this stage is for emerging leaders to comprehend the value of creating loving and caring cultures within their teams and be convinced of the need to care for those with whom they minister.

Wright has developed an excellent model for human resource development called the CARE plan, which cares for people's time and resources. It is built on four responsibilities of leaders: clarify expectations, agree on objectives, review progress, and equip for performance and growth.[58] These four basic requirements of leadership, with its memorable acronym, can enhance one's care for emerging leaders. Another objective is for developing leaders to become familiar with Wright's CARE plan and to use it as needed.

Leadership is primarily about empowering and serving others. Situational leadership and servant leadership are the main topics of discussion in this phase of the training. All leaders go through four predictable stages of development: low competence with high commitment, some competence with low commitment, moderate competence with variable commitment, and high competence with high commitment.[59] Leaders need to be responsive to these stages and adjust their style to provide more direction or support as needed.[60] The use of case studies, reflection questions, and

---

56. Ibid.
57. Ford with Osterhaus, "Leading from Within."
58. Wright, *Relational Leadership*, 160.
59. Blanchard and Fowler, *Self Leadership and the One Minute Manager*, 81–82.
60. Breen and Kallestad, *Passionate Church*, 111–29.

real-life examples will facilitate learning around these issues. One of the main objectives for this stage is to recognize the need to offer support or direction, depending upon the situation.

Along with situational leadership, leaders need to understand the dynamics of power, especially spiritual power. Christian leaders are called to say no to the alluring voices of power and prestige and participate in the divine dance of love and empowerment. When they do so, they reflect the inner life of God. L. Ford summarizes, "If the kingdom is Jesus' master thought, then servant leadership is his master principle."[61] Power in a Christian leader's life is to be used to promote self-control, to nurture confidence, to enhance communication, to inspire faith, to cultivate growth, and to facilitate competence.[62] One objective in this stage is for developing leaders to differentiate between natural and spiritual leadership.[63] Another power dynamic has been described by Hagberg as the six stages of power.[64] Understanding these stages, assessing one's level of power, and planning how to advance to the next level is how developing leaders can gain familiarity with these stages.[65]

To resist the temptation of destructive power and control, leaders must practice "radical discipline in their lives so they will not stumble or cause others to stumble."[66] They must practice toughness within themselves while exercising gentleness towards others.[67] This, according to Nouwen, is the discipline of "strenuous theological reflection," for only theological reflection allows leaders to discern critically where they are being led.[68] Together with reflection, leaders daily must take up the posture and attitude of a servant in order to serve and empower others. Foster recommends that leaders take a vow of service in the family, in the church, and in the world.[69] Another learning objective for this stage is to determine to be a

---

61. Ford, *Transforming Leadership*, 154.
62. Foster, *Challenge of the Disciplined Life*, 207–11.
63. Sanders, *Spiritual Leadership*, 29.
64. The six stages of power are powerlessness, by association, by symbols, by reflection, by purpose, and by gestalt; in Hagberg, *Real Power*.
65. Ibid. Assessments can be found at the end of each chapter in Hagberg's book.
66. Ford, *Transforming Leadership*, 146–47.
67. Ibid., 147.
68. Nouwen, *In the Name of Jesus*, 65.
69. Foster, *Challenge of the Disciplined Life*, 228–46.

servant-leader—one who lifts up and empowers others to become everything that God desires them to be.

Empowerment is the ultimate goal of effective leadership development. Stephen R. Covey defines leadership as "communicating to people their worth and potential so clearly that they come to see it in themselves."[70] Similarly, empowerment—the goal of the Trinity's leadership—entails raising people to new levels of achievement. It is about serving people and enabling them to fulfill their God-given destiny. This is the whole purpose of the dance of leadership: to serve and empower others with the love and grace received from entering into the dance of God.

FLEXIBLY, CREATIVELY, EFFORTLESSLY DANCING

While performance may be the final movement in the dance, it is not the final act in God's great drama. Having progressed through all four movements, leaders arrive back again at the center, the cool-down phase, which is also the warm-up phase for the next cycle. The capacities that leaders learn by practicing all twelve of these steps prepare them for great vision, greater responsibilities, and greater possibilities in the future. Having rehearsed the steps, leaders now are ready to invite others.

Like novice dancers, leaders begin by simply learning the steps. However, once they have mastered the movements, they gain confidence to dance with their own unique rhythms and steps, and are inspired to choreograph their own routine. Like professional dancers, their mastery leads to greater freedom to delight in the dance.

One of the qualities of the Trinity is the delight each member exhibits in the others. The Trinity invites leaders to participate in his dance for the sheer joy of participating together in accomplishing his dream. Those privileged to be in pastoral leadership at this exciting point in history have much to be joyful about. The number of people interested in discussing spiritual topics is rising.[71] God's Holy Spirit, moving across this great land, is awakening souls from their slumber, calling them into the dance. Pastoral leaders have the privilege of creating and dancing their unique dances in their local churches. My prayer is that the trinitarian movements described here will prove invaluable to those who courageously choose to lead in this

---

70. Covey, *8th Habit*, 98.
71. Bibby, *Restless Churches*, 85.

Part 3: Church-Based Strategies for the Trinitarian Leadership Dance

millennium. By following the movements of the Trinitarian Dance, leaders will experience greater ease, freedom, and joy in the task of leadership.

10

An Invitation from the Triune God

This last chapter provides a summary of the principles and concepts of the trinitarian leadership dance. It explains why a "doxological response" is an appropriate finale to the use of the Trinitarian Dance as a model for leadership development. It reviews the leadership crisis in the Canadian church, the theological foundation for using the Trinity's perichoretic dance as one's paradigm, and the challenge to the Canadian church to embrace this model to equip younger leaders for the challenges of leadership in Canada. It concludes with a benediction of grace, love, and hope for all Christ-followers who seek to participate with God in his transformational mission in Canada and beyond.

A DOXOLOGICAL RESPONSE

"Doxology" comes from two Greek words: *doxa*, meaning "honor and glory," *logos* meaning "the word" or "speaking."[1] Doxology is a fitting end to all talk about God. According to LaCugna, doxology is "remembrance of the past, lifting up of the present, and anticipation of our future with God."[2] Just as the Father, Son, and Holy Spirit glorify one another in perichoretic unity, humanity is created to worship and glorify the triune God. Velti-Matti Kärkkäinen defines "doxological response" as "participation in

---

1. BDAG, s.v. "doxology."
2. LaCugna, *God for Us*, 350.

and transformation into God rather than an attempt to know God *in se*."[3] To speak of the Trinity's transformational movements, then, is not only analogous to a dance but also doxological. LaCugna explains that since the Christian's vocation is to glorify God, doxology must be a way of life.[4] For her, the only proper mode of doing theology is doxology and adoration: "Soteriology culminates in doxology"[5]

In the final analysis, the Trinitarian Dance has everything to do with the Christian journey and life in the church. Knowledge about the Trinitarian Dance, however, is not the same as knowing the triune God. Moltmann explains, "For the Greek philosophers and the Fathers of the church, knowing meant something different: it meant knowing in *wonder*. By knowing or perceiving one participates in the life of the other . . . knowledge confers fellowship."[6] In other words, when training developing leaders using the movements of the Trinitarian Dance, one must ensure that they also learn how to let the Trinity live in and through them. Kärkkäinen refers to this type of knowledge as "doxological knowledge, knowing God by way of worshipping the triune God.[7] Doxology, then, is the purpose of transformational leadership development; God is glorified when kingdom-minded leaders are equipped.

Normally, doxology is associated with public worship in terms of patterns of prayers or short hymns that praise the Trinity. It is a short declaration of faith in the coequality of the three persons of the Holy Trinity. A common doxology in many Protestant traditions is this: "Praise God from Whom all blessings flow; Praise Him all creature here below; Praise Him above, ye Heavenly Host; Praise Father, Son, and Holy Ghost."[8] This doxology praises each member of the Holy Trinity and invites all of creation and heaven to join in the eternal worship of his Majesty. The last line of this particular doxology frames a summary of the ideas presented in this book.

---

3. Kärkkäinen, *Trinity*, 113.

4. LaCugna, *God for Us*, 342–48.

5. Ibid., 335.

6. Moltmann, *Trinity and the Kingdom*, 9.

7. Kärkkäinen, *Trinity*, xvi.

8. This particular doxology is sung every week in many Chinese churches. See also Ken, "Praise God from Whom All Blessings Flow."

An Invitation from the Triune God

Summary of Part 1: Praise to the Father

The Father longs to be glorified in the Canadian church. By examining the gap between reserved, indifferent Canadian Christians and bold, passionate, first-century Christians, this book has identified three sad realities of the Canadian church: Canadian Christians are shy about truth (chapter 1), towards others (chapter 2), and toward engagement in the world (chapter 3). Unlike the early Christians who gave their lives for the truth, reached out to others, and turned their world upside down, Canadian Christians have allowed too much of their culture to define who they are, where they belong, and how they behave. In order for the Father to be glorified, more must be done in the local church to develop kingdom-minded leaders.

Developing leaders means paying attention to both personal spirituality and leadership skills. Personal spirituality is expressed as Christians are formed into the image of Christ. The Father is committed to forming his character in his family members. Instead of being nice yet unresponsive, Canadian Christians are called to participate in what the Trinity is doing in Canada today. They must eschew a secular understanding of "tolerance as agreement" to embrace true tolerance in order to be able to dialog in the marketplace of ideas. Rather than being "passive theists" or "functional secularists," the Trinity is calling Canadian Christians to repent, to believe, and to witness to the kingdom of God that Christ established. Instead of blending into the fragmented, disconnected, cynical mosaic of postmodernity, the Father seeks those who will develop authentic, caring communities that will model and spread the message of hope to a despairing culture around them.

Rather than being satisfied with little or no influence in the world, God, in three persons, summons Canadian Christians to join him in being a transformative force and having a voice in the public square. Instead of membership in a local church being an optional afterthought, church membership must become a central practice for Canadian Christians seeking to belong to the family of God. Rather than being "pew potatoes," the Father expects every Canadian Christian to become active and involved in meaningful service in the Body of Christ. Instead of being lax in the practice of spiritual disciplines, God desires to meet with Canadian Christians in significant and personal ways through the practice of such disciplines. In contrast to the reserved, polite, and genteel approach to spiritual matters with which most Canadians are comfortable, God longs to infuse every believer with a passionate spirituality by filling them everyday with his Holy

Part 3: Church-Based Strategies for the Trinitarian Leadership Dance

Spirit. As kingdom-minded leaders are developed, these aforementioned symptoms of disease will be minimized and the Canadian church will become healthier, more vibrant, and gain more influence in Canadian society.

Summary of Part 2: Praise to the Son

By his incarnation, Jesus is the One who revealed the Father to this lost and desperate world. In the power of the Holy Spirit, he ministered to the Father on behalf of the world.[9] He also desires to see transformational leadership developed within the Canadian church, for he is the Lord of the dance. Together with the Father and the Spirit, he deserves all glory, honor, and praise for any positive changes in the Canadian milieu.

If the Canadian church is to regain lost ground, it must find new ways to develop leaders. The purpose of this book is to reverse the reticence that Canadian leaders have toward the Trinity's dance of love and life. Many Christian leaders are deaf to the tune of the leadership dance that the Trinity has orchestrated. Some never have been taught the steps. Others dance them rigidly and stiffly and do not understand the creativity intended in the dance. Still others dance them too loosely, not comprehending the purpose or pattern that the Trinity has intended for leadership.

Part 2 offered a theological rationale for using the Trinitarian Dance as a paradigm for leadership development in the Canadian church. The Trinity is a central tenet of the Christian faith. It is thoroughly biblical and has stood the test of time. It is a foundational truth that is knowable and makes a difference to leadership. Since Canadians do not have a strong sense of identity, participating in the Trinity's dance and being grounded in their identity as beloved sons and daughters offer Canadian Christians stability, security, and significance.

Part 2, then, presented *perichoresis*—the mutual indwelling of the Father, Son, and Holy Spirit—as the ideal way to develop twelve essential leadership micro-skills in emerging leaders. These skills were clustered into four movements: demonstration (chapter 5), choreography (chapter 6), orchestration (chapter 7), and performance (chapter 8). Progressively working through the four movements of the Trinity's leadership dance produces authentic leaders with a clear vision and the expertise to carry it out. The three steps of the demonstration phase—wholeness, balance, and trust—give emerging leaders credibility and moral authority to lead.

9. Anderson, *Shape of Practical Theology*, 40.

An Invitation from the Triune God

Starting with a clear vision, biblical values, and a realistic strategy (the steps of choreography), emerging leaders will gain a good understanding of their unique role in Christ's mission to the world. An ease with two-way communication, conflict resolution, and forgiveness (the steps of orchestration) will help developing leaders guard their heart and deepen their commitment to depend on the Father, just as Christ did when he walked on earth. Finally, those who create synergistic teams, exhibit care for their team members, and empower others to become all that they can be (the performance steps) reflect Christ's servant leadership. As emerging leaders follow the four movements and create their own dance in their particular ministry context, they take part in realizing God's transformative vision for themselves and their churches.

Summary of Part 3: Praise to the Holy Ghost

Despite numerous difficulties in the Canadian context, the Holy Spirit is active in the Canadian church today. Part 3 presented practical church-based strategies that join the Holy Spirit in developing leaders. By training emerging leaders in the steps of the Trinitarian Dance, pastors discover together with younger leaders new insights and details of God's transformational leadership dance. The Holy Spirit develops leaders both inwardly and outwardly as they practice together the steps of the dance and journey through the movements.

Learning the four movements is an ongoing process. The matrix of four movements surrounding a central warm-up phase shows how learning these steps is not linear but circular. After completing one rotation through the four movements, progressive cycles through these four phases result each time in deeper insights and greater proficiency. Leaders at any stage can benefit greatly from learning the four movements of the trinitarian leadership dance. As older leaders invest in emerging ones, new discoveries are made together about the intricacies and mystery of God's holy dance. The Holy Spirit is the one to be praised for all of these insights, for he is the person who is at work in the lives of his people and in his church in Canada.

A TRINITARIAN BENEDICTION

After the doxology, many worship services conclude with Paul's benediction to the Corinthian believers: "May the grace of the Lord, Jesus Christ;

the love of God; and the fellowship of the Holy Spirit, be with you all" (2 Cor 13:14). The invocation of God's blessing is significant due to its triadic formulation. Colin Kruse observes, "It is the only place in the New Testament where God the Father, Son, and Holy Spirit are explicitly mentioned together with such a blessing."[10] This trinitarian blessing provides the scaffold for concluding thoughts on the Trinitarian Dance as a paradigm for leadership development in the Canadian church.

The Grace of the Lord Jesus Christ

Christ's grace is completely undeserved for Canadian leaders who have been busy stomping on toes and remaining deaf to the Spirit's call to the dance, yet the grace of the Lord Jesus Christ is overwhelmingly generous. The grace of the Lord refers to his favor and goodwill bestowed on all of humanity. Christ's grace provides access both to the Father's love and to the Spirit's empowerment. Due to Christ's grace, leaders experience the Father's acceptance and delight in them as his children. Receiving the grace of the Lord Jesus Christ is necessary since leaders will face challenges, opposition, and resistance to change. Grace also is needed for times of failure, since such times will come. However, despite the weaknesses or failings of Canadian leaders, Christ's grace is sufficient (2 Cor 12:9).

Christ's grace is not only for church leaders but also for all Canadians, who are starving for grace. The lost need grace, for it "contains the essence of the gospel as a drop of water contains the image of the sun."[11] Unfortunately, many in the church experience so much ungrace that they are turned off. Philip Yancey explains, "I rejected the church for a time because I found so little grace there. I returned because I found grace nowhere else."[12] The Body of Christ needs to experience grace in order to become a message of grace and hope to a despairing and cynical culture. The Canadian church needs authentic models living in God's *shalom* by being filled with the Holy Spirit, exercising balance in daily life, and being trustworthy in everything. Emerging leaders are hungering for grace. They need older, wiser mentors who will share with them the grace of the Lord Jesus Christ and help them discover the steps of the Trinitarian Dance so that they can follow in his footsteps.

10. Kruse, *Second Epistle of Paul to the Corinthians*, 224.
11. Yancey, *What's So Amazing about Grace?*, 13.
12. Ibid., 16.

An Invitation from the Triune God

The Love of God

The very love that the Father enjoys with the Spirit and the Son he extends to all his children. Just as the Father, Son, and Holy Spirit delight and enjoy one another's company, similarly the Father delights in his children—not for what they do but simply for who they are. The Father loves his children unconditionally and longs to embrace them with his all-encompassing love. The Father wants Canadian leaders to know the complete acceptance of his love, for they will find peace in his loving embrace.

Canadian leaders need to experience satisfaction not in the bustle of many activities but solely in hearing and obeying the Father's loving call. Adopted into God's family, leaders do not need to strive to obtain the Father's blessing or acceptance; rather, they can rest secure in his covenantal love. Free from insecurity or drivenness, Canadian leaders can be confident in their position as sons and daughters of the King. They have no reason to fear when opposition or criticism emerges, for they are secure in the knowledge of the Father's unfailing love for them. Even in the midst of dark valleys, they trust that God cares for them and will work out all things together for good (Rom 8:28).

Sociologists have a theory of the looking glass self.[13] People become what the most important person in their life thinks that they are. Canadian leaders' lives would significantly change if they only truly believed and received the love of the Father. If in all their endeavors, Canadian leaders imagined the Father lovingly looking down on them, delighting in their efforts, enjoying their company, and being proud of their trust, the results would be transformational.

The Fellowship of the Spirit

The word "fellowship" comes from the Greek word *koinonia*.[14] Just as the Father, Son, and Holy Spirit experience a mutual indwelling of one another, Paul desired for the Corinthian Christians to experience a close fellowship with God through the indwelling presence of the Holy Spirit. Canadian leaders also must experience this close fellowship with God by walking with the Spirit each and everyday (Gal 5:16). This is the Spirit's consuming

---

13. "Looking Glass Self."
14. BDAG, s.v. "koinonia."

desire: to empower and enable believers to live a life of righteousness through reliance on him (Rom 8:1–17).

Canada requires leaders who engage with modern culture with the wisdom of the Holy Spirit. The Canadian church needs leaders who are led by the Spirit rather than motivated by unmet personal needs. Instead of seeking to control others, Canadian leaders must develop self-control by the power of the Holy Spirit (2 Tim 1:7). In lieu of timidity and apathy, Canadian leaders must allow the Holy Spirit to explode in their hearts and guide them in all their ways.

Be with You All

The trinitarian movements are not just for leaders but for all disciples who long to experience more of God's presence in their own daily walk. All are called to lead their own lives and to respond to the rhythms and movements of the Trinity. All Christ-followers have been entrusted with Christ's Great Commission (Matt 28:18–20). All can learn the movements of the dance and model their lives in such a way as to inspire others to follow. All have been invited, as Buxton has expressed, "to dance with God in the darkness of this world."[15]

The purpose of this entire discussion has been to inspire, motivate, and equip Canadian leaders to develop leaders in their own context. Unpacking the intricacies of *perichoresis* is not meant to be merely a theological exercise; rather, it encompasses the means to achieving a deeply transformative understanding of the nature of leadership development. The proper role of theology is to lead people to a deeper love for God, to contrition over sin, and to a transformed life. Thomas à Kempis cautions theologians and practitioners alike: "What does it profit thee to enter into deep discussion concerning the Holy Trinity, if thou lack humility, and be thus displeasing to the Trinity? For verily it is not deep words that make a man holy and upright; it is a good life which maketh a man dear to God."[16]

---

15. Buxton, *Dancing in the Dark*, 4.
16. Kempis, *Imitation of Christ*, I.I.3.

An Invitation from the Triune God

A GREAT COMMISSION

In closing, I share this story of my encounter with an elderly gentleman who helped to design the Canadian flag. I met this man while visiting The People's Church in Toronto in 1997. He described how he had entered into the Great Canadian Flag Debate of 1964 with a design that was very similar to the design that was eventually adopted. The solitary red maple leaf, he explained, represented the triune God. One maple leaf, consisting of three fronds, represented one God in three persons. The red color represented the blood of Christ. In his design, the two side borders were blue[17]—not red, like the final version—which represented the prayer of the Fathers of Confederation: "He shall have dominion from sea to sea" (Ps 72:8).[18] This man's design was adopted by the New Democratic Party and thereby defeated Lester B. Pearson's preferred three-branch proposal.[19] From this design, my new friend explained, came the red and white maple leaf flag that Canadians honor today. I have never looked at the Canadian flag the same way since. Now, whenever I gaze at it I remember the Trinity. It is my prayer that the Trinitarian Dance presented herein will contribute to raising up more kingdom-minded leaders so that the Trinity might reign increasingly from sea to sea in this great nation of Canada and beyond.

17. Bist, *Canada Return to Your Roots*.
18. Motz, ed., *Reclaiming a Nation*, 13.
19. For more information on the Canadian flag, see "Birth of the Canadian Flag."

Bibliography

Adams, Michael, with Amy Langstaff and David Jamieson. *Fire and Ice: United States, Canada, and the Myth of Converging Values.* Toronto: Penguin, 2003.
Amanatides, Margaret. "Women Risking for the Kingdom: A Historical Look at Women in Missions." Lecture presented at a Toronto Chapter Meeting of Christians for Biblical Equality, Danforth Mennonite Church, Toronto, May 26, 2005.
Anderson, Neil. *Victory Over the Darkness: Realizing the Power of Your Identity in Christ.* 2nd ed. Ventura, CA: Regal, 2000.
———, and Charles Mylander. *Setting Your Church Free: A Biblical Plan to Help Your Church.* Ventura, CA: Regal, 1994.
Anderson, Ray Sherman. *An Emergent Theology for Emerging Churches.* Downers Grove, IL: InterVarsity, 2006.
———. *The Shape of Practical Theology: Empowering Ministry with Theological Praxis.* Downers Grove, IL: InterVarsity, 2001.
"Apostles' Creed." Christian Classics Ethereal Library. Online: http://www.ccel.org/creeds/apostles.creed.html.
Argot Language Center. "I Am Canadian: Canadian Commercial by Molson." Online: http://www.r-go.ca/canadian_commercial_molson.htm.
Augsburger, David W. *Caring Enough to Forgive: True Forgiveness.* Scottdale, PA: Herald, 1981.
Augustine, Saint. *On the Holy Trinity.* Translated by Arthur West Haddan. In vol. 3 of *Nicene and Post-Nicene Fathers*, series 1, edited by Philip Schaff. 1873. Reprint, Grand Rapids: Eerdmans, 1956. Christian Classics Ethereal Library. Online: http://www.ccel.org/ccel/schaff/npnf103.
Bandy, Thomas G. *Coaching Change: Breaking Down Resistance, Building Up Hope.* Nashville: Abingdon, 2000.
Baril, Alain, and George Mori. "Leaving the Fold: Declining Church Attendance." *Canadian Social Trends* no. 22 (Fall 1991). Statistics Canada. Online: http://www5.statcan.gc.ca/olc-cel/olc.action?ObjId=11-008-X19910021373&ObjType=47&lang=en&limit=0.
Barna, George. *The Power of Vision: How You Can Capture and Apply God's Vision for Your Ministry.* Ventura, CA: Regal, 1992.
Barth, Karl. *The Doctrine of the Word of God.* Translated by G. T. Thomson. Edited by G. W. Bromiley and T. F. Vol. 1 of *Church Dogmatics.* Torrance. 2 vols. Edinburgh: T. & T. Clark, 1936.

Bibliography

Bauer, Walter, Frederick W. Danker, W. F. Arndt, and F. W. Gingrich. *Greek- English Lexicon of the New Testament and Other Early Christian Literature*. 2nd ed. Chicago: University of Chicago Press, 1979.

Bibby, Reginald W. *The Bibby Report: Social Treads Canadian Style*. Toronto: Stoddart, 1995.

———. *The Boomer Factor: What Canada's Most Famous Generation Is Leaving Behind*. Toronto: Bastian, 2006.

———. *Mosaic Madness: The Poverty and Potential of Life in Canada*. Toronto: Stoddart, 1990.

———. *Restless Churches: How Canada's Churches Can Contribute to the Emerging Religious Renaissance*. Toronto: Novalis/Saint Paul University, 2004.

———. *Restless Gods: The Renaissance of Religion in Canada*. Toronto: Stoddart, 2002.

———. *There's Got to Be More: Connecting Churches and Canadians*. Winfield, BC: Wood Lake Books, 1995.

———. *Unknown Gods: The Ongoing Story of Religion in Canada*. Toronto: Stoddart, 1993.

Bilezikian, Gilbert. *Community 101: Reclaiming the Church as Community of Oneness*. Grand Rapids: Zondervan, 1997.

"Birth of the Canadian Flag." Canadian Heritage. Online: http://www.pch.gc.ca/eng/1363358734450/1363344743820.

Bist, George Matthais. *Canada Return to Your Roots: Give All Glory to God*. Toronto: George M. Bist, 1996.

Blanchard, Ken, and Susan Fowler. *Self Leadership and the One Minute Manager: Increasing Effectiveness through Situational Self Leadership*. New York: HarperCollins, 2005.

Boff, Leonardo. *Trinity and Society*. Maryknoll, NY: Orbis; Tunbridge Wells, Kent, UK: Burns & Oates, 1988.

Bowen, Kurt Derek. *Christians in a Secular World: The Canadian Experience*. Montréal, QC: McGill-Queen's University, 2004.

Boyd, Gregory A. *Repenting of Religion: Turning from Judgment to the Love of God*. Grand Rapids: Baker, 2004.

Bray, Gerald L. "Out of the Box: The Christian Experience of God in Trinity." In *God the Holy Trinity: Reflections on Christian Faith and Practice*, edited by Timothy George, 37–56. Grand Rapids: Baker Academic, 2006.

Breen, Mike, and Walter Kallestad. *The Passionate Church: The Art of Life-Changing Discipleship*. Colorado Springs, CO: Cook Communications Ministries, 2005.

Brown, Francis, S. R. Driver, and Charles A. Briggs. *Hebrew and English Lexicon of the Old Testament*. Oxford: Clarendon, 1951.

Buckingham, Janet Epp. *Withering Rights: Religious Freedom in Canada*. Markham, ON: Faith Today Pub., 2004.

Buxton, Graham. *Dancing in the Dark: The Privilege of Participating in the Ministry of Christ*. Carlisle, Cumbria, UK: Paternoster, 2001.

———. "On the Trinitarian Doctrine of *Perichoresis*: The Spirit in the Divine, the Human and the Physical." Paper presented at "Participating in the Ministry of Christ: A Trinitarian Theology of Ministry," MacMaster Divinity College, Hamilton, ON, June 19, 2007.

———. "Participating in the Ministry of Christ: A Trinitarian Theology of Ministry." Lecture, McMaster Divinity College, Hamilton, ON, June 18–22, 2007.

Bibliography

———. *The Trinity, Creation and Pastoral Ministry: Imaging the Perichoretic God.* Paternoster Theological Monographs. Milton Keynes, UK: Paternoster, 2005.

Canadian Mental Health Association. "Reflections on Youth Suicide." Online: http://www.canadiancrc.com/PDFs/CMHA_mh_pamphlet_29.pdf.

"Canadian Multiculturalism: An Inclusive Citizenship." Citizenship and Immigration Canada. Online: http://www.cic.gc.ca/english/multiculturalism/citizenship.asp.

Canadian Multiculturalism Act. R.S.C., 1985, c. 24 (4th Supp.). (S.C., 1988, c. 31, assented to July 21, 1988).

"The *Canadian Multiculturalism Act.*" Parole Board of Canada. Online: http://www.pbc-clcc.gc.ca/infocntr/multi-eng.shtml.

"Canadian Population Surpasses 35 Million." CBC News, September 26, 2013. Online: http://www.cbc.ca/news/canadian-population-surpasses-35-million-1.1869011.

Canavan, Francis. *The Pluralist Game: Pluralism, Liberalism, and the Moral Conscience.* Lanham, MD: Rowman and Littlefield, 1995.

Chapman, Alan. "Abraham Maslow's Hierarchy of Needs Motivational Model." Online: http://www.businessballs.com/maslow.htm.

———. "Management Skill Set Assessment." Online: http://www.businessballs.com/managerskillsetassessment.pdf

Civil Marriage Act. S.C., 2005, c. 33.

Cladis, George. *Leading the Team-Based Church: How Pastors and Church Staffs Can Grow Together into a Powerful Fellowship of Leaders.* San Francisco: Jossey-Bass, 1999.

Clinton, J. Robert. *The Making of a Leader.* Colorado Springs, CO: NavPress, 1988.

Cloud, Henry, John Sims Townsend. *Boundaries: When to Say Yes, When to Say No to Take Control of Your Life.* Grand Rapids: Zondervan, 1992.

Cohen, Andrew. *The Unfinished Canadian: The People We Are.* Toronto: McClelland and Stewart, 2007.

Collins, James C. *Good to Great: Why Some Companies Make the Leap—and Others Don't.* New York: HarperBusiness, 2001.

Compton, Sophia. "Theophilus of Antioch and the 'Two Hands of God.'" *Theandros* 4/2 (Winter 2006/2007).

Covey, Stephen R. *The 8th Habit: From Effectiveness to Greatness.* New York: Free Press, 2004.

———, with Rebecca R. Merrill. *The Speed of Trust: The One Thing That Changes Everything.* New York: Free Press, 2006.

Crabb, Larry. "God's Square Dance: 5 Questions for Larry Crabb." *Leadership Journal*, July 13, 2004. Online: http://www.christianitytoday.com/le/2004/july-online-only/cln40713.html.

Cusick, Michael J. "A Conversation with Eugene Peterson." *Mars Hill Review* 3/3 (Fall 1995) 73–90. Online: http://www.leaderu.com/marshill/mhr03/peter1.html.

De Pree, Max. *Leadership Is an Art.* New York: Currency/Doubleday, 2004.

———. *Leading Without Power: Finding Hope in Serving Community.* San Francisco: Jossey-Bass, 1997.

DeGraaf, Darren. "Personal Growth Plan Handbook." Baptist Convention of Ontario and Quebec. Online: http://www.baptist.ca/pastors/pastorsfiles/personal_growth_plan_june_07.pdf.

Edgar, Brian. *The Message of the Trinity.* The Bible Speaks Today. Downers Grove, IL: InterVarsity, 2004.

Edwards, Gene. *The Divine Romance.* Auburne, ME: Christian Books Publishing, 1984.

Bibliography

Erickson, Millard J. *Christian Theology*. 1-vol. ed. Grand Rapids: Baker, 1983.

———. *Making Sense of the Trinity: Three Crucial Questions*. Grand Rapids: Baker, 2000.

Falikowski, A. "What's Your Conflict Management Style." Online: http://www.webhome.idirect.com/~kehamilt/ipsyconstyle.html.

Fee, Gordon D. *The First Epistle to the Corinthians*. NICNT. Grand Rapids: Eerdmans, 1987.

Fiddes, Paul S. *Participating in God: A Pastoral Doctrine of the Trinity*. London: Darton, Longman, and Todd, 2000.

Ford, Kevin Graham, and James P. Osterhaus. *The Thing in the Bushes: Turning Organizational Blind Spots into Competitive Advantage*. Colorado Springs, CO: Pinon, 2001.

Ford, Leighton. "Helping Leaders Grow." In *Leaders on Leadership: Wisdom, Advice, and Encouragement on the Art of Leading God's People*, edited by George Barna, 123–48. Ventura, CA: Regal, 1997.

———. *Transforming Leadership: Jesus' Way of Creating Vision, Shaping Values, and Empowering Change*. Downers Grove, IL: InterVarsity, 1991.

———, with Jim Osterhaus. "Leading from Within." Leadership retreat, Blowing Rock, NC, November 10–14, 2003.

Foster, Richard J. *Celebration of Discipline: The Path to Spiritual Growth*. 3rd ed. San Francisco: Harper Collins, 1998.

———. *The Challenge of the Disciplined Life: Christian Reflections on Money, Sex, and Power*. San Francisco: Harper & Row, 1985.

Frazee, Randy. *The Christian Life Profile Assessment Tool: Workbook*. Grand Rapids: Zondervan, 2005.

———. *The Connecting Church*. Grand Rapids: Zondervan, 2001.

Garcia, Benche. "The Life of a Newcomer to Canada." In *Canada's New Harvest: Helping Churches Touch Newcomers*, edited by Brian Seim, 17–21. Toronto: SIM Canada, 1997.

George, Timothy, editor. *God the Holy Trinity: Reflections on Christian Faith and Practice*. Grand Rapids: Baker Academic, 2006.

———. "Introduction." In *God the Holy Trinity: Reflections on Christian Faith and Practice*, edited by Timothy George, 9–16. Grand Rapids: Baker Academic, 2006.

Giles, Kevin. *The Trinity and Subordinationism: The Doctrine of God and the Contemporary Gender Debate*. Downers Grove, IL: InterVarsity, 2002.

Gire, Ken. *The Divine Embrace*. Wheaton, IL: Tyndale House, 2003.

Goleman, Daniel. *Emotional Intelligence: Why It Can Matter More than IQ*. London: Bloomsbury, 1996.

Green, Joel B., Scot McKnight, and I. Howard Marshall, editors. *Dictionary of Jesus and the Gospels*. IVP Bible Dictionary Series 6. Downers Grove, IL: InterVarsity, 1992.

Grenz, Stanley J. and John R. Franke. *Beyond Foundationalism: Shaping Theology in a Postmodern Context*. Louisville: Westminster John Knox, 2001.

Gruenler, Royce Gordon. *The Trinity in the Gospel of John: A Thematic Commentary on the Fourth Gospel*. Grand Rapids: Baker, 1986.

Guthrie, Shirley C. *Christian Doctrine*. Rev. ed. Louisville: Westminster John Knox, 1994.

Hagberg, Janet O. *Real Power: Stages of Personal Power in Organizations*. Rev. ed. Minneapolis: Winston, 1984.

———, and Robert A. Guelich. *The Critical Journey: Stages in the Life of Faith*. Salem, WI: Sheffield, 1989.

Bibliography

Hahn, Todd, and Jim Osterhaus. *The Mentoring Tree: A Leadership Legacy of Leighton Ford*. Charlotte, NC: Leighton Ford Ministries, 2006.
Hamblin, Michael. "Evangelical Resources on True Tolerance." Online: http://www.evangelicalresources.org/tolerance.shtml.
Harris, R. Laird, Gleason L. Archer Jr., and Bruce K. Waltke, editors. *Theological Wordbook of the Old Testament*. Chicago: Moody, 1980.
Hart, Archibald. "Minister's Personal Growth." Lecture, Fuller Theological Seminary, Pasadena, CA, October 10, 2005.
———. "Minister's Personal Growth: The Assertiveness Inventory." Lecture, Fuller Theological Seminary, Pasadena, CA, October 5, 2005.
———. "Minister's Personal Growth: Burnout Checklist." Lecture, Fuller Theological Seminary, Pasadena, CA, October 14, 2005.
———. "Minister's Personal Growth: Checklist for Self-Differentiation." Lecture, Fuller Theological Seminary, Pasadena, CA, October 11, 2005.
———. "Minister's Personal Growth: Intimacy Scale for Couple Work." Lecture, Fuller Theological Seminary, Pasadena, CA, October 10, 2005.
———. "Minister's Personal Growth: Self-Rating Anxiety Scale." Lecture, Fuller Theological Seminary, Pasadena, CA, October 14, 2005.
———. "Minister's Personal Growth: Stress Test." Lecture, Fuller Theological Seminary, Pasadena, CA, October 13, 2005.
———, and Rick Blackmon. "Minister's Personal Growth: Sexual Behavior of Ministers." Lecture, Fuller Theological Seminary, Pasadena, CA, October 10, 2005.
Herrington, Jim, Mike Bonem, and James Furr. *Leading Congregational Change: A Practical Guide for the Transformational Journey*. San Francisco: Jossey-Bass, 2000.
Hybels, Bill. *Courageous Leadership*. Grand Rapids: Zondervan, 2002.
InterVarsity Christian Fellowship. "Evangelism Code of Ethics." Online: http://www.intervarsity.org/evangelism/article_item.php?article_id=1503.
Irvine, Andrew. "Clergy Well-Being: Seeking Wholeness with Integrity." Online: http://sites.utoronto.ca/caringforclergy/Copy%20of%20good%20edit%20of%20chapters%201%20-%2028.pdf.
Jenson, Robert W. *The Triune Identity: God According to the Gospel*. Philadelphia: Fortress, 1982.
Jewett, Paul D. K. *God, Creation, and Revelation: A Neo-Evangelical Theology*. Grand Rapids: Eerdmans, 1991.
John of Damascus, Saint. *Exposition of the Orthodox Faith (De Fide Orthodoxa)*. Translated by S. D. F. Salmond. In vol. 9 of *Nicene and Post-Nicene Fathers*, series 2, edited by Philip Schaff and Henry Wace. 1899. Reprint, Grand Rapids: Eerdmans, 1955. Christian Classics Ethereal Library. Online: http://www.ccel.org/ccel/schaff/npnf209.iii.html.
Johnson, Darrell W. *Experiencing the Trinity*. Vancouver, BC: Regent College Publishing, 2002.
Johnson, J. K. "Sir John A. Macdonald." Rev. by Tabitha Marshall. *The Canadian Encyclopedia*. Historica Foundation, 2013. Online:
Kärkkäinen, Veli-Matti. *The Trinity: Global Perspectives*. Louisville: Westminster John Knox, 2007.
Keillor, Garrison. "Faith at the Speed of Light." *Time*, June 14, 1999. Online: http://www.time.com/time/archive/preview/0,10987,991211,00.html.
Kempis, Thomas à. *The Imitation of Christ*. Uhrichsville, OH: Barbour and Co., 1984.

Bibliography

Ken, Thomas. "Praise God from Whom All Blessings Flow." Online: http://www.cyberhymnal.org/htm/p/r/praisegf.htm.

Keyes, Dick. *Beyond Identity: Finding Yourself in the Image and Character of God.* Ann Arbour, MI: Servant Books, 1984.

Kimball, Dan. *The Emerging Church: Vintage Christianity for New Generations.* Grand Rapids: Zondervan, 2003.

King, Martin Luther, Jr. "I Have a Dream." Delivered August 28, 1963. Online: http://www.americanrhetoric.com/speeches/mlkihaveadream.htm.

Kotter, John P. *Leading Change.* Boston: Harvard Business School Press, 1996.

Kouzes, James M., and Barry Z. Posner. *Credibility: How Leaders Gain and Lose It, Why People Demand It.* San Francisco: Jossey-Bass Publishers, 1993.

Kraft, Gerald C., and R. Murray A. Jarman. "How Current Trends Impact the Church." In *Transforming our Nation*, edited by Murray Moerman, 333–63. Richmond, BC: Church Leadership Library, 1998. Online: http://www.outreach.ca/ OC6-Resources/download/TON/15%20Chapter%2010.pdf.

Kruger, C. Baxter. *The Great Dance: The Christian Vision Revisited.* Vancouver, BC: Regent College Publishing, 2000.

Kruse, Colin. *The Second Epistle of Paul to the Corinthians.* Tyndale New Testament Commentaries. 1987. Reprint, Grand Rapids: Eerdmans, 1998.

Kuhn, Robert. "Death of a Dream, Birth of a Vision." In *Mentoring Leaders: Wisdom for Developing Character, Calling, and Competency*, by Carson Pue, 115–21. Grand Rapids: Baker, 2005.

LaCugna, Catherine Mowry. *God for Us: The Trinity and Christian Life.* San Francisco: HarperSanFrancisco, 1991.

Lawson, Kevin, and Joan Carter. "Personal Ministry Integration: Christian Life Assessment Scale." Lecture, Canadian Theological Seminary, Regina, SK, October 1993.

———. "Personal Ministry Integration: Spiritual Well-Being, Ellison, 1983." Lecture, Canadian Theological Seminary, Regina, SK, October 1993.

Lencioni, Patrick. *The Five Dysfunctions of a Team: A Leadership Fable.* San Francisco: Jossey-Bass, 2002.

Leupp, Roderick. *Knowing the Name of God: A Trinitarian Tapestry of Grace, Faith, and Community.* Downers Grove, IL: InterVarsity, 1996.

Lewis, C. S. *Mere Christianity.* New York: Macmillan, 1960.

———. *Surprised by Joy.* 1st American ed. New York: Harcourt, Brace, 1956.

Locke, John L. *The Devoicing of Society: Why We Don't Talk to Each Other Anymore.* New York: Simon & Schuster, 1998.

Logan, Robert E., and Sherilyn Carlton, with Tara Miller. *Coaching 101: Discover the Power of Coaching.* St. Charles, IL: ChurchSmart Resources, 2003.

"Looking Glass Self." Wikipedia. Online: http://www.wikiwand.com/en/Looking_glass_self.

Malphurs, Aubrey. *Values-Driven Leadership: Discovering and Developing Your Core Values for Ministry.* Grand Rapids: Baker, 1996.

Marshall, I. Howard, et al., editors. *New Bible Dictionary.* 3rd ed. Downers Grove, IL: InterVarsity, 1996.

Maxwell, John. *The 17 Indisputable Laws of Teamwork: Embrace Them and Empower Your Team.* Nashville: T. Nelson, 2001.

———. *The 21 Irrefutable Laws of Leadership: Follow Them and People Will Follow You.* Nashville: T. Nelson, 1998.

Bibliography

McGrath, Alister. "The Doctrine of the Trinity: An Evangelical Reflection." In *God, the Holy Trinity: Reflections on Christian Faith and Practice*, edited by Timothy George, 17–36. Grand Rapids: Baker Academic, 2006.

McNeal, Reggie. *Revolution in Leadership: Training Apostles for Tomorrow's Church*. Nashville: Abingdon, 1998.

———. *A Work of Heart: Understanding How God Shapes Spiritual Leaders*. San Francisco: Jossey-Bass, 2000.

"Some Thoughts on the Value of Religion." The Meeting House. Online: http://www.themeetinghouse.ca.

Mehrabian, Albert. "Personality & Communication: Psychological Books & Articles of Popular Interest." Online: http://www.kaaj.com/psych/.

Middleton, Mark. "Perspectives on the World Christian Movement." Lecture, Mississauga Chinese Baptist Church, Mississauga, ON, May 30, 2006.

Moerman, Murray. "Church Planting: The Key to Growth." In *Reclaiming a Nation: The Challenge of Re-Evangelizing Canada by the Year 2000*, edited by Arnell Motz, 83–106. Richmond, BC: Outreach Canada/Church Leadership Library, 1990.

———, editor. *Transforming Our Nation: Empowering the Canadian Church for a Greater Harvest*. Richmond, BC: Church Leadership Library, 1998.

Moltmann, Jürgen. *The Crucified God: The Cross of Christ as the Foundation and Criticism of Christian Theology*. Translated by R. A. Wilson and John Bowden. London: Harper & Row, 1974.

———. *God in Creation: A New Theology of Creation and The Spirit of God*. Translated by Margaret Kohl. San Francisco: Harper & Row, 1985.

———. *The Trinity and the Kingdom: The Doctrine of God*. Translated by Margaret Kohl. San Francisco: Harper & Row, 1981.

"Mother Teresa—Biographical." Nobel Media AB, 2014. Online: http://nobelprize.org/nobel_prizes/peace/laureates/1979/teresa-bio.html.

Motz, Arnell, editor. *Reclaiming a Nation: The Challenge of Re-Evangelizing Canada by the Year 2000*. Richmond, BC: Outreach Canada/Church Leadership Library, 1990.

Neuhaus, Richard John. *The Naked Public Square: Religion and Democracy in America*. Grand Rapids: Eerdmans, 1984.

The Catholic Encyclopedia. New York: Robert Appleton Co., 1908. Online: http://www.newadvent.org/cathen/.

Nicole, Roger R. "The Meaning of the Trinity." In *Standing Forth: Collected Writings of Roger Nicole*. Fearn, Ross-shire, Scotland: Christian Focus, 2002.

"Notorious Mount Cashel Orphanage to Close." CBC News, November 27, 1989. Online: http://archives.cbc.ca/IDC-1-70-1951-12676-11/disasters_tragedies/twt.

Nouwen, Henri. J. M. *Behold the Beauty of the Lord: Praying with Icons*. Notre Dame, IN: Ave Maria, 1987.

———. *Creative Ministry*. Garden City, NY: Doubleday, 1971.

———. *Life of the Beloved: Spiritual Living in a Secular World*. New York: Crossroad, 1992.

———. *In the Name of Jesus: Reflections on Christian Leadership*. New York: Crossroad, 1989.

Ogden, Greg. *Transforming Discipleship: Making Disciples a few at a Time*. Downers Grove, IL: InterVarsity, 2003.

"Ontario Voter Turnout a Record Low." CBC News, October 11, 2007. http://www.cbc.ca/canada/ontariovotes2007/story/2007/10/11/ov-turnout-071010.html.

Bibliography

Packer, J. I. *Knowing God*. London: Hodder & Stoughton, 1973.

"Patron Saints Index." The Catholic Forum. Online: http://www.catholicforum.com/saints_index.html.

Petersen, Jim. *Lifestyle Discipleship: The Challenge of Following Jesus in Today's World*. Colorado Springs, CO: NavPress, 1993.

Pinnock, Clark H. *Flame of Love: A Theology of the Holy Spirit*. Downers Grove, IL: InterVarsity, 1996.

Posterski, Don. *Where's a Good Church?* Winfield, BC: Wood Lake Books, 1993.

———, and Reginald Wayne Bibby. *The Emerging Generation: An Inside Look at Canada's Teenagers*. Toronto: Irwin, 1985.

Prabhu, R. K., and U. R. Rao, editors. *The Mind of Mahatma Gandhi*. Rev. ed. Ahemadabad, India: Jitendra T. Desai/Navajivan Trust, 1967. Online: http://www.mkgandhi.org/momgandhi/main.htm.

Pue, Carson. *Mentoring Leaders: Wisdom for Developing Character, Calling, and Competency*. Grand Rapids: Baker, 2005.

Queendom: The Land of Tests. Online: http://www.queendom.com.

Quinn, Robert E. *Deep Change: Discovering the Leader Within*. San Francisco: Jossey-Bass, 1996.

Rahner, Karl. *The Trinity*. Translated by Joseph Donceel. New York: Herder and Herder, 1970.

Ratzinger, Joseph. *Church, Ecumenism, and Politics: New Essays in Ecclesiology*. New York: Crossroad, 1988.

Remin, Rod. "Hebrew Exegesis." Lecture delivered at Canadian Theological Seminary, Regina, SK, 1995.

Ridley, Charles R., Steven J. Goodwin, and Robert E. Logan, editors. *Overcoming Resistance to Change*. Saint Charles, IL: ChurchSmart Resources, 2003.

Righton, Barbara. "Maclean's Poll 2006: How We Live." *Maclean's Magazine*. "Top Stories." Online: http://www.macleans.ca/topstories/polls/article.jsp?content=20060701_130281_130281.

Russel, Letty M. *Church in the Round: Feminist Interpretation of the Church*. Louisville: Westminster John Knox, 1993.

Sanders, J. Oswald. *Spiritual Leadership*. Chicago: Moody, 1967.

Sayers, Dorothy L. *The Whimsical Christian: 18 Essays*. New York: Macmillan, 1978.

Scazzero, Peter, with Warren Bird. *The Emotionally Healthy Church: A Strategy for Discipleship That Actually Changes Lives*. Grand Rapids: Zondervan, 2003.

Schwarz, Christian A. *Color Your World with Natural Church Development: Experiencing All That God as Designed You to Be*. St. Charles, IL: ChurchSmart Resources, 2005.

———. *The 3 Colors of Ministry: A Trinitarian Approach to Identifying and Developing Your Spiritual Gifts*. St. Charles, IL: ChurchSmart Resources, 2001.

Seamand, Stephen. *Ministry in the Image of God: The Trinitarian Shape of Christian Service*. Downers Grove, IL: InterVarsity, 2005.

Seim, Brian. Interview by the author. Mississauga, ON, July 5, 2006.

"Solar Temple: A Cult Gone Wrong." CBC News, November 27, 1989. Online: http://archives.cbc.ca/IDD-1-70-501/disasters_tragedies/solar_temple.

Song, Minho. "Patterns of Religious Participation among the Second Generation Koreans in Toronto: Towards the Analysis and Prevention of the 'Silent Exodus.'" PhD diss., Trinity Evangelical Divinity School, 1999.

Bibliography

Stackhouse, John G., Jr. *Canadian Evangelicalism in the Twentieth Century: An Introduction to Its Character*. Toronto: University of Toronto Press, 1993.

Stanley, Paul D., and J. Robert Clinton. *Connecting: The Mentoring Relationships You Need to Succeed in Life*. Colorado Springs, CO: NavPress, 1992.

Statistics Canada. "Employed Labour Force Having a Usual Place of Work or No Fixed Workplace Address by Mode of Transportation: 2001 Counts for Both Sexes, for Canada, Provinces and Territories—20% Sample Data." http://www12.statcan.ca/english/census01/products/highlight/Pow/RetrieveTable.cfm?Lang=E&T=601&GH=4&D1=1&SC=1&SR=1&S=99&O=A.

Statistics Canada. "Population, Urban and Rural, by Province and Territory. Online: http://www.statcan.gc.ca/tables-tableaux/sum-som/l01/cst01/demo62a-eng.htm.

Statistics Canada. "2001 Census—Release 4—December 10, 2002." Online: http://www12.statcan.ca/english/census01/release/release4.cfm.

Statistics Canada. "2003 General Social Survey on Social Engagement, Cycle 17: An Overview of Findings—Chart 3. How Canadians Describe Their Sense of Belonging to Canada, by Province of Residence, 2003." Online: http://www.statcan.ca/english/freepub/89-598-XIE/2003001/Figures/chart3.htm.

Stetson, Brad, and Joseph G. Conti. *The Truth about Tolerance: Pluralism, Diversity, and the Culture Wars*. Downers Grove, IL: InterVarsity, 2005.

Stiller, Brian C. *From the Tower of Babel to Parliament Hill: How to Be a Christian in Canada Today*. Toronto: HarperCollins, 1997.

Sweet, Leonard. *Soul Salsa: 17 Surprising Steps for Godly Living in the 21st Century*. Grand Rapids: Zondervan, 2000.

———. *Summoned to Lead*. Grand Rapids: Zondervan, 2004.

Swenson, Richard A. *Margin: How to Create the Emotional, Physical, Financial, and Time Reserves You Need*. Colorado Springs, CO: NavPress, 1992.

Taylor, Daniel. *Is God Intolerant?: Christian Thinking about the Call for Tolerance*. Wheaton, IL: Tyndale House, 2003.

Tenney, Merrill C, and J. D. Douglas, editors. *The New International Dictionary of the Bible: Pictorial Edition*. Rev. ed. Grand Rapids: Zondervan, 1987.

Todd, Douglas. "B.C. Psychotherapist Tries to Make Virtue a Reality in age of Cynicism." *Vancouver Sun*, January 6, 2000. Online: http://article.wn.com/view/2000/01/06/BC_psychotherapist_tries_to_make_virtue_a_reality_in_age_of_/.

Torrance, Thomas F. *The Christian Doctrine of God: One Being, Three Persons*. Edinburgh: T. & T. Clark, 1996.

———. *Trinitarian Perspectives: Toward Doctrinal Agreement*. Edinburgh: T. & T. Clark, 1994.

Townend, Steward. *How Deep the Father's Love for Us*. Kingsway's Thankyou Music, 1995.

Volf, Miroslav. *After Our Likeness: The Church as the Image of the Trinity*. Grand Rapids: Eerdmans, 1998.

———. *Free of Charge: Giving and Forgiving in a Culture Stripped of Grace*. Grand Rapids: Zondervan, 2005.

"Voter Turnout at Federal Elections and Referendums." Elections Canada. Online: http://www.elections.ca/content.asp?section=pas&document=turnout&lang=e&textonly=false.

Wainwright, Arthur William. *The Trinity in the New Testament*. London: SPCK, 1962.

Wainwright, Geoffrey. *Doxology: The Praise of God in Worship, Doctrine, and Life*. New York: Oxford University Press, 1980.

Bibliography

Walsh, Gary. "Striving for Relevance in a Changing Nation." In *Transforming Our Nation: Empowering the Canadian Church for a Greater Harvest*, edited by Murray Moerman, 305–32. Richmond, BC: Church Leadership Library, 1998.

Warren, Rick. *The Purpose Driven Church: Growth without Compromising Your Message and Mission*. Grand Rapids: Zondervan, 1995.

Webber, Jeremy H. A. *Reimagining Canada: Language, Culture, Community, and the Canadian Constitution*. Montreal: McGill-Queen's University Press, 1994.

Willard, Dallas. *The Divine Conspiracy: Rediscovering Our Hidden Life with God*. San Francisco: HarperSanFrancisco, 1998.

―――. *The Great Omission: Reclaiming Jesus's Essential Teachings on Discipleship*. San Francisco: HarperSanFrancisco, 2006.

―――. *Hearing God: Developing a Conversational Relationship with God*. Downers Grove, IL: InterVarsity, 1984.

―――. *Renovation of the Heart: Putting On the Character of Christ*. Colorado Springs, CO: NavPress, 2002.

―――. *The Spirit of the Disciplines: Understanding How God Changes Lives*. San Francisco: Harper & Row, 1988.

―――, with Keith Matthews. "Spirituality and Ministry." Lecture, Fuller Theological Seminary, at Mater de la Rosa Retreat Center, Sierra Madre, CA, June 5, 2003.

"William (Billy) F. Graham." Billy Graham Evangelistic Association. Online: http://billygraham.org/about/biographies/billy-graham/.

Wilson, Sandra D. *Released from Shame: Moving Beyond the Pain of the Past*. Rev. ed. Downers Grove, IL: InterVarsity, 2002.

Wood, Chris. "1988 Maclean's Decima Poll." *Maclean's*, January 2, 1989.

Wright, Walter C. *Relational Leadership: A Biblical Model for Influence and Service*. Carlisle, Cumbria, UK: Paternoster, 2000.

Yancey, Philip. *What's So Amazing about Grace?* Grand Rapids: Zondervan, 1997.

Zizioulas, John D. *Being as Communion: Studies in Personhood and the Church*. Crestwood, NY: St. Vladimir's Seminary Press, 1985.

www.ingramcontent.com/pod-product-compliance
Lightning Source LLC
Chambersburg PA
CBHW050816160426
43192CB00010B/1777